C000216143

CROWN ··· ···DEVON

THE HISTORY OF
S. FIELDING & Co.

BY
SUSAN HILL

JAZZ PUBLICATIONS

Published in 1993 by

Jazz Publications Limited
Civic Hall
Rother Street
Stratford Upon Avon
Warwickshire
Telephone : 0789 298362

ISBN 0 9516525 2 4

Print and Origination by Flaydemouse, Yeovil, Somerset

This book is dedicated to the memory of Abraham and Reginald Fielding - two gentlemen of the Potteries

Contents

Acknowledgements

Photographs and material reproduced and utilised from the Crown Devon archives, held at the County Record Office, Stafford are by courtesy of the Stoke-on-Trent City Museum and Art Gallery.

Photographs and material reproduced from the Pottery Gazette, the Pottery and Glass Record and Tableware International publications are by kind permission of Tableware International magazine.

Photographs and material reproduced from the Fielding family scrapbook are by kind permission of Mary Fielding.

Reproduction of photograph of 1908 Stoke football team is by courtesy of Wade Martin, historian and statistician to Stoke City Football Club.

Reproduction of photograph of Mucklestone Races is by courtesy of Harvey Stonehewer.

The items that appear in the book were photographed by courtesy of :
Wyn Bates, Freda Boulton, Len and Pam Brown, Joe and Doreen Calvert, John and Katherine Cox, Linda Ellis, Mary Fielding, Julian Gilbert and Cherie Brooks, Dennis Harwood and John Walford, David and Lisa Heaton, Judith and Jake Jones, Liz and Rhodri Lewis, Jean and John McNally, Ron and Valerie Morgan, Paddy Owens, Graham Panico, Brian Parkes and Gill Tombs, Peter Sharp, Stoke-on-Trent City Museum and Art Gallery, Harvey and Anne Stonehewer, Bill and Joan Thomas, Vivian and Martin Truran, Doris Waite, Diane and John Wright.

Sincere thanks to Brian Parkes for artwork of the backstamps.

Photography

All photographs by Rod Fawkes Photography, Cwmbran for Jazz Publications Limited.

Important Note

Every effort has been made to provide accurate and comprehensive information. However, due to the incompleteness of the source material, inaccuracies and omissions have inevitably been made. The author and publisher will not be held responsible for any losses incurred because of information contained in this book. Any readers who wish to offer further information are invited to write to the author via the publisher's address.

Preface

I have long been an admirer of the pottery produced by S. Fielding & Co but disappointed by the lack of information available. Hence, my first objective was to 'fill the gap'. However equally important was a desire to set the record straight in view of the disparaging remarks sometimes heard about Crown Devon. Far from being *'Poor Man's Worcester'* or *'Imitation Carlton'*, Crown Devon had a style of its own and often set, rather than followed, the popular trends.

The research has been fascinating although often frustrating due to the incompleteness of the records. I have found the history of the Fielding family and the development of their pottery more rivetting than any fictional saga.

However, the most enjoyable aspect of the work has been the opportunity to meet several of the people who worked at the Devon Pottery. Their recollections, told with enthusiasm and much affection, have brought Crown Devon to life again. As such, I offer my heartfelt thanks to Bill Bannister, Freda Boulton, Arnold Kennerley, Harvey Stonehewer and Bill Thomas for their time, valuable assistance and friendly welcome.

I wish to gratefully acknowledge the assistance of Kathy Niblett of the Stoke-on-Trent City Museum and Art Gallery who has always found time to answer my questions, suggest avenues of research and generally assist the project. I must also record with appreciation the information supplied by Doreen Bagguley, Wade Martin and Tom Wilcox.

Finally, I offer my warmest thanks to Mary Fielding who has supported this project in word and action and has provided me with a unique insight into the business.

I hope other Crown Devon fans will enjoy this book and that it will also bring a justly deserved recognition of the firm's achievements. As Fielding's proudly proclaimed in their advertisements, Crown Devon wares certainly have

'Charm and Distinction'.

Susan Hill

Simon Fielding

A Family Firm

A history of the Fielding family and development of the Devon
Pottery

The history of the Fielding family is interwoven with the history of Crown Devon. Through four generations, they built the firm with forward-thinking and investment into one of the premier fancy ware manufacturers.

Small Beginnings

Simon Fielding, the founder of the firm, was born in 1827. He came to Trentham to work for the Duke of Sutherland on his estate at Trentham Hall. An acknowledged authority and judge on dogs and poultry, his reputation spread not only throughout Britain but also the Continent.

His son, Abraham, was born in 1855 at Middleton, Lancashire. Educated at St Peters School, Stoke and at Thomas Hemming's School in Copeland Street, Abraham passed the Cambridge Local Examination in 1870.

In the same year, he began his apprenticeship as a colour maker at a small colour mill on the River Blythe at Cresswell, later to become the Blythe Colour Works. It was probably owned by Herbert Bailey at this time but was subsequently acquired by Simon and, in 1872, Abraham was placed in charge of the business which now traded as S. Fielding.

In the Spring of 1878, Simon Fielding provided the money to start three practical pottery men on a manufacturing career. The principle two of these were Frederick Hackney and J. Kirkham, both of whom had previously worked in the Fancy Goods Department at Wedgwood's for many years. The business was located at the Railway Pottery, Sutherland Street, Stoke and traded as both Hackney, Kirkham & Company and F. Hackney & Company. Simon's investment seems to have been used to improve the site and facilities, as reported in the Pottery Gazette of May 1878 following a visit to the firm :

> We have much pleasure in recording a visit to the above manufactory, the propri-
> etors of which we may state are young potters having but recently entered into the
> business. The premises are large, giving plenty of scope for enterprise and energy.
> An additional oven is being erected, new machinery put down and extensive
> rearrangements made. Altogether the outlook is very promising.

The Fielding colour mill supplied the pottery with colours but the day to day management was left to the three men. Abraham visited the works regularly for settlement of accounts and, on one such visit, towards the end of 1879, arrived to find the bailiffs in possession of the premises.

He decided to pay off the debts and become a pottery manufacturer himself. Abraham showed considerable courage in undertaking this venture since, at 24, he had no detailed knowledge of pottery production and there was no pottery school at which it might be formally gained. His experience of colour manufacture and the friends he had made in the pottery industry stood him in good stead. However, the firm was built primarily upon Abraham's capacity for hard work.

In those first years, he found it necessary not only to do his own warehouse and office work, but also to fire his own ovens. For some time, the colour manufacturing business at Cresswell operated simultaneously. However, the development of the Railway Pottery required Abraham's entire attention resulting in the sale of the colour mill, to Pigott and Scarratt.

Abraham Fielding was, above all, a practical man actively involved in all aspects of the business and with strong views on how to achieve success. Under his guidance, the business prospered and grew rapidly resulting in a progression of extensions to the works.

By April 1883, a range of warehouses, workshops and two kilns had been added together with new machinery which enabled an increasingly diverse range of production. New steam jiggers and stoves were under installation, in early 1884, when disaster struck. On February 6th, fire swept through the factory and, although every effort was made, it was not brought under control for several hours. By that time, the principal buildings had been wrecked with only the outer walls remaining. A large quantity of stock and machinery was destroyed with the loss estimated at between £3,000 and £4,000. However, the factory was quickly reconstructed and, within two months, the rebuilding had been completed.

The same year, the firm began to enjoy the patronage of the Duchess of Sutherland. This may have been due to the links between the Duke and Duchess of Sutherland and the Fielding family, established through Simon's previous employment with them. It is likely that samples were sent regularly to Trentham Hall from which the Duchess could make her purchases although she also visited the works from time to time.

The business continued to prosper and, in October 1887, the Pottery Gazette reported that :

> Messrs Fielding have recently erected a new kiln and are now building a large three-storied building to accommodate over eighty hands to enable them to meet their continually increasing business.

In May 1888, progress was again dramatically cut short when fire struck the works once more. The alarm was raised by employees living in houses adjacent to the factory and fire engines belonging to the North Staffordshire Railway Company were quickly on the scene. In spite of their efforts, the fire burnt out of control and the buildings were completely gutted with everything contained in the workshops being totally destroyed. Damage was estimated at £4,000. Obviously, production was at a standstill for some months with the factory inoperable until August.

Abraham turned the misfortune of the fire to the advantage of the business in the resultant rebuilding. In a staged construction programme, he actively involved himself in planning the best arrangement of buildings to meet the working requirements of a modern earthenware manufactory.

By July 1890, the works boasted a new biscuit oven fired on an entirely new principle. By regulating the flow of gases, it was possible to maintain a more even temperature which, it was claimed, provided great savings in fuel, time in firing and, maintenance and repair costs. It is interesting to note that a new line of business resulted from these improvements as the firm patented the oven modification and made it available to other manufacturers under licence.

The early autumn witnessed the erection of a large glost oven based on the same principle whilst two enamel kilns were completed early the following year. This gave the factory seven of the largest kilns in the Potteries used exclusively for the production of decorated earthenware. During the same period, six cottages adjoining the works were acquired and converted into workshops equipped with the most modern machinery available.

Perhaps the most dramatic change came in 1892 when permission was obtained to close Sutherland Street and absorb the thoroughfare, together with the properties, into the factory site. This provided land for the construction of printing and decorating departments together with warehouses and showrooms. In the following year, a glaze mill was built which enabled the firm not only to manufacture glaze for themselves but also to sell it to other pottery manufacturers. The final stage of these major developments was unsurprising considering Abraham's background. With the decision to build a colour mill, the factory became almost self-sufficient, except for raw materials.

The fundamental principle underlying the development plan was that progress was best achieved by a strict cohesion of departmental working. However, within this overall framework, Abraham was motivated by two primary considerations. Firstly, to improve efficiency and thus maximise production, and secondly, to secure the health and comfort of the workforce, particularly the women who were specially cared for. This resulted in the introduction of labour-saving machinery wherever possible together with more efficient manual working practices.

The following extract, from an extensive report on the improvements made, appeared in the Pottery Gazette of January 1898 :

> *Another perfect example of labour-saving appliance is a revolving dryer for glazes. The dipper places the articles, as they are dipped, on the shelves of a large revolving wheel. The revolutions are regulated so that he has just time to fill each shelf as it comes level with him, before it passes out of reach. We understood this series of shelves on a wheel takes about 20 to 25 minutes to revolve. By the time the shelf reaches the side opposite to that on which the dipper fills it, the glaze is quite dry, and the pieces are dexterously removed from the shelf by a youth, who, of course, works at the same rate as the dipper.*

Notable improvements also included the provision of an abundant supply of water in each room, the introduction of a pipework system for the disposal of waste and the installation of lifts for transporting ware between the kilns and the decorating department. The workrooms, particularly those of the decorators, were light, airy and well-ventilated with fans being fitted wherever necessary. Clean air was also actively sought after in another area, that of the colour groundlayers. In addition to the usual respirators, each worker was provided with a boxed-in case which placed a glass sheet between him and the item being coloured with a fan carrying all the fumes out of the back of the case.

The co-ordinated standard of efficiency which the factory had achieved attracted considerable envy from their competitors. At the same time, the consideration shown to the workforce resulted in a good, almost family, spirit with Abraham as the strict but fair patriarch being held in high esteem. Abraham's view of his workforce as an extended family and their reciprocation is best demonstrated by two events.

The first, in May 1900, was at the conclusion of a strike which had affected the entire pottery industry. The Pottery Gazette reported :

> A Good Example - Messrs S. Fielding & Co., Railway Pottery, Stoke showed their appreciation of the settlement of the dispute with their workpeople one Saturday last month in a practical and commendable way. Invitations were issued to each of the workers by the principal, Mr A. Fielding, to a picnic at the hotel. Upwards of 200 employees presented themselves and sports of various characters were indulged in in the field adjoining, after which justice was done to a substantial tea. Immediately after tea, dancing commenced and an enjoyable evening was spent.

Three years later, the employees were invited to join in the celebrations for the silver wedding of Abraham and his wife. Tea was served to over 250 in the afternoon and was followed by a presentation. The gifts consisted of a silver salver and a silver spirit kettle together with an illuminated address executed by Mr Wagstaffe, an artist at the works. The address read :

> Presented to Mr and Mrs A. Fielding, together with the accompanying silver salver, by the employees of Messrs S. Fielding & Co., Railway Pottery, Stoke-on-Trent, on the occasion of the celebration of their silver wedding. April 22 1903. A token of sincere esteem and regard from a body of appreciative workpeople to one who has ever had at heart the interest and welfare of his employees.

In responding to the presentation, Abraham said that much as he valued the costly present, he would prize the address most because of the kindly sentiments it expressed.

In 1905, having grown to almost five times the size at which Abraham had taken it over, S. Fielding & Co. became a limited company. Registered with a capital of £13,000 in £1 shares, the subscribers were A. Fielding, A.R. Fielding, J. Sayer, A.G. Richardson, F. Green, R.W. Day and Mrs E.M. Keeling - the first three of these becoming the directors.

Later in the same year, having witnessed a success that he could have scarcely imagined when he made his initial investment twenty-seven years previously, Simon Fielding died at the age of 78.

From Strength to Strength

It is a little ironic that the company's marketing policy was so successful that the wares became better known than the name of the pottery which produced them, with mail often addressed simply to "*the makers of Crown Devon*". Consequently, in 1911, it was decided to avoid any further confusion by changing the factory name from the Railway to the Devon Pottery.

In September 1911, Abraham was elevated to the judicial bench and also demonstrated once again his good opinion of his workforce in a practical way. On this occasion, he presented seven female and twelve male employees with gifts commemorating their long service with the firm. Each person received a photograph of Abraham in his hunting costume together with a large flowerpot and pedestal bearing the inscription :

> *A Souvenir. For 21 years continuous service in the employ of Messrs S. Fielding & Co.*

The trade press reported that Abraham had made a *"happy little speech"*, saying that :

> *He had been thinking over the matter in his quiet moments and had come to the conclusion that these were people who thought not simply of the £sd question but who showed an appreciation of loyal service and had aims which were apparently a little above simple money making.*

The final occurrence of this eventful month was, unfortunately, not a happy one. On September 19th, a disastrous fire broke out in the three-storey main building containing painting and decorating shops, offices and warehouses. The outbreak was discovered by a night kilnsman who immediately gave the alarm to the members of the company's private fire brigade living in cottages nearby. However, the fire had taken such a firm hold that the Stoke and Fenton brigades as well as the North Staffordshire Locomotive brigade were also summoned. Although the firemen attacked the flames from all points, their efforts made little impression and, fanned by a strong breeze, the fire spread rapidly. The building was soon ablaze from end to end and, within an hour, the roof fell in. Ultimately, it was almost completely destroyed with only the walls and the ovens left standing. Fortunately, the brigades were successful in preventing the fire from spreading to the adjoining warehouses and cottages.

The value of the damage to stock and property was estimated at £15,000. No time was lost in arranging for the rebuilding of the works with Mr Wood, the architect, on the scene settling preliminaries even before all the firemen had left.

The company employed between 400 and 500 people at this time, most of whom were temporarily thrown out of work by the fire. As might be expected, Abraham took prompt and generous steps to alleviate the effects on his workforce. He offered to let those in need of money draw wages and pay a little back each week once they restarted work.

Again, full advantage was taken of the rebuilding necessitated by the fire and important improvements were made. The result was a well-appointed factory and decorating shops, installed with the most up-to-date machinery and accessories, together with an extension to the factory showroom.

In April 1913, King George V and Queen Mary made an extended visit to Stoke-on-Trent visiting a selected number of factories, one of which was the Devon Pottery.

The Devon Pottery welcomes King George V and Queen Mary in April 1913

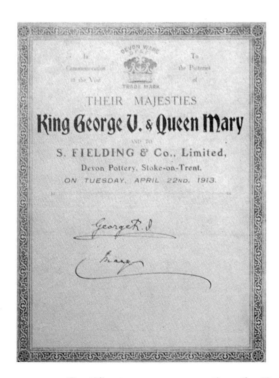
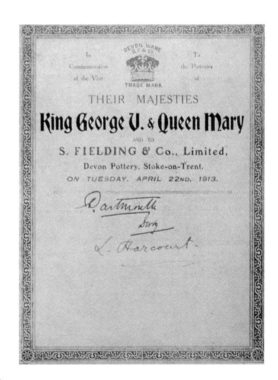

Certificates commemorating the Royal visit

Although their stay was limited to about ten minutes, they were shown as many of the different stages of manufacture as possible. After being greeted by Abraham on their arrival, the royal couple parted company. The Queen was shown the printing shop before moving on to the aerographing shop where she expressed considerable interest in the ventilation arrangements, asking numerous questions. In the meantime, the King went down to the kilns where he enquired into the working conditions of the firemen and inspected trials drawn to show him the ware in the process of firing. Finally, a display had been arranged showing each stage in the manufacture of Devon ware from the raw clay to the finished article.

As part of the arrangements for the royal visit, an exhibition was organised by the various pottery companies, including Fielding's. This was held at the King's Hall, Stoke-on-Trent where it was visited by the King and Queen. Following a period of well-attended public access, the exhibition moved to Harrods in London where Queen Mary took the opportunity of a more leisurely viewing of the displays. The royal seal of approval proved a good advertisement for the pottery manufacturers involved and many people followed the Queen's example by purchasing goods from the exhibition.

The outbreak of war in 1914 did not have an immediate effect - in fact, to a large extent, it was business as usual. However, as time passed, the shortage of manpower became increasingly serious. All levels of staff were affected including Abraham's nephew, Francis Edward Taylor, who had been in charge of the Potting Department of the firm before joining the 1/5th North Staffordshire Regiment.

One of the principle ways in which the firm surmounted these difficulties was by their well-established and far-sighted policy of applying advances in technology. Hence, in 1917, a gas-fired Dressler tunnel enamelling kiln was installed. This had a weekly capacity equal to 34 four-mouth intermittent kilns and, as it replaced only twelve such kilns, the weekly capacity was increased almost threefold.

In addition to his overall management of the Devon Pottery, Abraham continued to actively involve himself in the business, social and, to a lesser extent, political life of the community.

In 1919, the Pottery and Glass Trades Benevolent Institution embarked on a scheme of technical education for sales men and women engaged in the retail trades. Each successful examination candidate was entitled to a weeks visit to the Potteries, free of cost, to give them first hand experience of production methods. The Devon Works actively participated in this scheme with the visitors being taken on a detailed guided tour of all manufacturing processes. After watching handpainting and lustring together with an inspection of the Dressler kiln, afternoon tea was served. On their departure, each visitor was given a gift of two small pieces of lustred ware as a souvenir.

As has previously been noted, Abraham was a practical man who had a detailed knowledge of the operation of his works. This was highlighted when he was asked to take part in a symposium on 'Unestimated Losses in Pottery Manufacture' organised by the Ceramic Society in January 1920. In a strong speech, he stated that losses occurred for a variety of reasons amongst which were a lack of attention to detail, carelessness, oversight, insufficient supervision and want of knowledge. Whilst acknowledging the failures of the workforce in particular instances, he put the onus squarely onto the owners to show a positive attitude to their factories and to develop efficient working practices through first hand experience.

The company in general, and Abraham in particular, had always engendered great loyalty from their staff. In the death of James Sayer from influenza in 1922, Fielding's lost an invaluable and trusted member of the firm. Born in Yorkshire, he had joined Abraham as a young man in a junior position and had worked his way up to be a director and the Company Secretary.

A key factor of the general election of 1923 was the question of free trade versus protection. This had the effect of dividing the pottery manufacturers into two opposing camps. Feelings ran so high that Abraham took part in active electioneering for the first time when he joined Percy Shelley on the platform to support the Liberal Free Trade candidate.

Abraham's abiding love of sport was acknowledged by two presentations in the mid-1920's. The first in 1924 was a gold and enamel badge from the Stoke Victoria Athletic Club in recognition of his services as Chairman of the club, President of the North Staffordshire Harriers, Vice-President of the Staffordshire A.A.A. and official judge under the Midland Counties A.A.A.

The Pottery Gazette, quoting Cox's Potteries Annual described him thus :

> *Even at 70 years of age, Mr Fielding is open to swim a couple of lengths with men forty years his junior. Considering his age and his weight he is something of a wonder in his agility. His chief hobbies are golfing, hunting and motoring. .... As for his motoring, it is said that his speedometer could tell some tales which, in the public interest, it will perhaps be better not to attempt to relate.*

Two years later, the North Staffordshire Harriers presented Abraham with a large framed portrait of himself in recognition of his services to athletics in North Staffordshire. Abraham amused the gathered company by recalling the bicycle races from the West End Hotel at Stoke to Rugeley and back. Thousands of people congregated along the route to watch the competitors on their old-fashioned, high wheel bicycles; the police keeping the spectators off the footpaths so that they did not impede the cyclists!

Earlier the same year, 1926, Abraham was elected President of the North Staffordshire Branch of the Commercial Traveller's Association, following Major Wedgwood into that office. In his acceptance speech, he again took the opportunity of berating the industry for its negative approach to the problems they faced. He discounted price-cutting and protection policies as solutions to falling trade and suggested that it was more energy that was required. The Pottery Gazette reported that :

> *He would like to see more of the spirit that obtained in America and which enabled America to export her productions in spite of high wages. In America men put their backs into their businesses and even proprietors of businesses put their shoulders to the wheel, at times with their jackets off. He himself had been connected*

Abraham Fielding on his Penny Farthing, 1876

with the pottery trade since 1873 and he had fired his own ovens and drawn them and was happy in doing so. At that time he knew many manufacturers, but there were few who went to work at nine in the morning and he believed they accomplished far more then than they did nowadays, sitting in an office pushing a bell and sending someone to tell someone else to do something.

The Devon works progressed well given the general economic climate of the time. However, it was not without setbacks, particularly when fire struck again in April 1926. The fire was confined to a flint grinding mill which was completely destroyed with damages estimated at between £2,000 and £3,000. Fortunately, the numerous offers of assistance received, pending the rebuilding of the mill, ensured that the factory could continue operating unimpeded and consequently no output or jobs were lost.

Having been an active huntsman for many years, Abraham finally had to forgo this favourite pastime when he suffered a heart attack in 1927. Considerable concern was obviously expressed about his health but, after a period of rest, his natural vitality re-asserted itself and he was soon back at the works.

Happier times were enjoyed in November 1928 when over 300 staff and employees gathered at Fenton Town Hall to commemorate a triple event. Firstly, Reginald, Abraham's grandson had attained his majority; secondly Abraham and his wife were celebrating their golden wedding anniversary and thirdly, the Devon Pottery had reached its jubilee.

Mr J.T. Broome, the Commercial Manager, presented Reginald with a dressing case on behalf of the firm's employees. In his accompanying speech, he said that everyone at the works was proud of 'Mr Reg' ; some of the older members had watched him grow up and remembered him being brought to the works when only a few months old and being carried round the warehouses with great pride by his grandfather.

Abraham also took the opportunity of making gifts to his grandson. The first was an insurance policy for £500 taken out when Reginald was born to mature on his coming of age. The second was the fulfilment of a bargain made some years previously which was that if Reginald could remain teetotal and a non-smoker until he was 21, Abraham would give him £100.

Following Reginald's thanks, Mr F. Turner the Works Manager, congratulated Abraham and his wife on their golden wedding and on the fifty years of the Devon Pottery. Presentations were then made of a solid gold Eversharp pencil to Abraham and a cut glass flower bowl to Mrs Fielding. Mrs Fielding also received, from one of the firm's oldest women workers, a beautiful hand-embroidered linen tablecloth.

It is worth noting that, far from taking life easy, Abraham was still a magistrate, Chairman of the Mechanical Committee of the British Pottery Manufacturer's Federation as well as being President of the Commercial Traveller's Association, North Staffordshire Branch. Amongst his other business interests was a silk mill at Macclesfield, a colour manufacturing business in the Potteries, and he was chairman of The Manor Engineering Co. Ltd, a local firm of pottery, colliery and motor engineers.

Abraham Fielding at the hunt

Three generations : Abraham and his wife Mary (centre), Alec Ross (left) and Reginald (right). 1928

With his son and grandson actively participating in the firm, supported by a strong and loyal management team, Abraham finally decided to reduce his involvement in the day to day management of the company in 1930. Helping to partially fill the gap left, Mr George Barker joined the firm as Sales Director after twenty-four years as a travelling representative.

An expansion of the works also took place in 1930 when the Era Art Pottery started production of cellulose wares. Wholly owned by Fielding's and situated on the Devon Pottery site, Era was a decorating house only, using biscuit wares manufactured by Crown Devon. Separate ranges of shapes and patterns were designed for Era which were predominantly ornamental articles. However, there was also a limited interchange between the companies; some Era shapes were used for Crown Devon patterns whilst the cheaper range of Crown Devon Sutherland figurines were decorated at Era. The Era Art Pottery continued trading until 1947 although very little was produced after 1940.

The inevitable end of an era arrived on March 23rd 1932. Abraham Fielding died, at the age of 77, following a period of indifferent health. Describing him as a man of courage and pertinacity, the obituary in the Pottery Gazette went on to record his remarkable achievements as a sportsman, businessman and respected member of the community. The funeral was held at the Parish Church, Blurton and was attended by representatives of practically every section of the corporate life of the district. It is a fitting tribute to Abraham that memories of him have been long-lasting. Many fond recollections are still recounted today with his methods of 'commuting' from home to the works forming the basis of many of the stories, including cycling along the frozen canal. However, the most vivid recollections are those of him riding his favourite grey horse, often stopping to give the local children a short ride with him.

Abraham's only son, Arthur (Alec) Ross, now became the third generation of the family to head the company. Born in 1880, he was educated at Manor House College, Hastings. It was not only in business that he followed in his father's footsteps, also being a popular and successful figure in sporting circles. Over the years, his activities had ranged from football and cricket to steeplechasing and polo.

In his younger days he played for the prominent Trentham Nomads Football Club and was a member of the team which won the Sentinel Cup in 1901. He subsequently played outside-right for Stoke Football Club (later Stoke City FC), making 109 first team appearances and scoring 12 goals. Regularly described as an ebullient player and a good dribbler with a fine body swerve, he also played for Nottingham Forest and West Bromwich Albion before retiring in 1915. Perhaps the best story of Ross was that when West Bromwich came to sign him, he was out hunting to hounds on his father's estate.

As a cricketer he had played for a long period with the Trentham Club where he gained the reputation of being an extremely useful fast bowler and batsman. For many years, he was a member of the North Staffordshire Hunt and, in 1913, won the North Staffordshire Heavyweight Hunt Steeplechase. He also achieved considerable success as a polo player. However, by the time he took over at Fielding's, his involvement was mainly confined to that of an enthusiastic spectator, particularly as a supporter of Stoke City Football Club.

1908 Stoke Football team with Alec Ross (front, left hand side)

Our Greetings go round the World in ever-widening Circles

Christmas 1938

Company Christmas card, 1938, reflecting Reginald's involvement in the export markets

It is worth reiterating that the links between Stoke City Football Club and the Fielding family were long-standing. Abraham had been a Chairman of the club whilst both Ross and Ned Taylor had played for them. This close association was recognised when a road near the ground was named after the family.

The Fielding family's love of sport was echoed at the works where cricket and football teams were formed by members of the staff. Encouraging these activities, the company rented a pitch for the football team whilst Ross bought Australian-style caps for the cricket team.

The Thirties also saw Reginald playing an increasingly prominent role. As a director and the Commercial Manager, he took a special interest in the overseas markets and his extensive travels built up and cemented important business relationships world-wide. His visits included Canada, Australia, New Zealand, America and South Africa. Exhibitions of Crown Devon products were often staged in conjunction with these visits, such as in the principal cities of Australia during 1938. This was so successful that almost all the articles shown were sold and consequently re-ordered in their entirety.

Again, success was tempered by sadness when the firm lost another long-serving employee with the death of John Thomas Broome in March 1937. He had been with the company since boyhood, a total of nearly 51 years, holding the position of Departmental Manager at the time of his death. As well as responsibility for all overseas orders, for many years it was one of his duties to act as receptionist to every pottery dealer visiting the works.

In keeping with their consistent record of being abreast of the times in mechanisation, extensive plans for development were prepared in 1938. These included the construction of a new glost tunnel oven. However, the outbreak of war in 1939 prevented the immediate implementation of these plans.

The War Years and After

On the cessation of hostilities, the whole factory site was surveyed and a major plan approved for complete reconstruction. This included implementation of the previously proposed new glost oven and replacement of the old Dressler tunnel kiln by a modern gas-fired enamel kiln. All the main casting shops were entirely re-equipped and modernised, electrically powered jiggers replaced those driven by an old steam engine and modern drying stoves were installed. The programme was finally completed in 1950.

Unfortunately, Ross was not to witness the completion of these plans. After a prolonged period of ill-health, he died in February 1947, aged 66. Apart from his extensive sporting interests, his life-long enthusiasm had been for farming which would have been his chosen career given different circumstances. He had established a herd of pedigree dairy shorthorns at the Leasows, Hilderstone in 1919 and achieved considerable success with them. In 1926, he went on to build up one of the finest herds of pedigree Jerseys at the Old Mill House, Blurton. He was also well-known for breeding hunters and had won prizes at agricultural shows in this field. Interestingly, the workers at Crown Devon benefited from his farming activities as Ross was able to provide the daily milk supply for the dipping house workers and aerographers from

1949, erection of new gas-fired glost oven inspected by Ned Taylor

1949, new gas-fired enamel kiln installed to replace old Dressler kiln

1949, new casting shop with mono pump installation

1949, a corner of the cup making and turning shop

his herd. His business interests also went beyond his position as Chairman of S. Fielding & Co. Ltd. He was Chairman of C.J. Baines & Co. Ltd and proprietor of Messrs William Boardman & Co, both colour manufacturers.

Ross was succeeded by his son, Reginald, who had been actively involved in the company for many years. Attached to the Territorials (Royal Artillery), he was called up immediately war was declared and served for six years. On his return, he was the driving force behind the planning of the factory reconstruction and supervised all stages of the work.

In January 1948, another significant loss occurred with the death of the director, Frederick Turner. Highly respected as a potter, he had joined the pottery some 32 years previously as General/Works Manager when one of his first responsibilities was supervising the installation of the Dressler tunnel oven. The new Works Manager was Alfred Tomkinson who joined the firm from Paragon China.

The company was dealt a harsh blow on May 16th 1951 when fire again swept through the factory destroying some 44,000 square feet of floor space. The fire, which broke out in the first floor aerographing shop, was discovered at 3 am. Within the first half-hour, it had enveloped the whole of the centre building and burned so fiercely that the glare in the sky could be seen in many parts of Stoke.

All Fire Brigade stations in the city were mobilised but the work of the firemen was severely hampered by a strong breeze which fanned the flames and put surrounding properties at risk. All available water supplies were pressed into service including a high-powered pump which was operated from the nearby canal. Although the fire was soon surrounded by eight powerful jets, aided by a turntable water tower, it was still not brought under control until 6.30 am. Such serious damage was caused to the entire premises that building inspectors were called in to give advice on the safety of the remaining walls with the result that some were demolished immediately.

In the final reckoning, the decorating, aerographing and printing shops, glost and biscuit warehouses, showrooms and offices were completely gutted. The slip house, new dipping house, glost oven and new enamel kiln were unscathed although the electrical equipment to both kilns was destroyed. Large stocks of earthenware goods, destined for export, were lost at an estimated value of £8,000 to £10,000. A significant portion of these goods were musical novelties awaiting the delivery of the musical movements prior to their despatch. By a cruel irony, the shipment of these musical movements arrived at the factory just a few days after the fire.

Some 320 employees were temporarily thrown out of work by the destruction and, conscious of this, an official statement of advice was quickly issued by the firm. It read :

> *Will all workpeople who have not done so, please report at the Labour Exchange as a temporary measure? They will then be notified, direct or through the Press, when work can be resumed. Emergency arrangements will be made as soon as possible. Should employees be directed to other firms, we ask them to get in touch with us first, as we hope to start the glost oven shortly and a limited amount of decorating.*

A view of part of the devastation caused by the fire in 1951

Reconstruction in progress following the fire, 1951

Staff outing to Mucklestone Races in the 1950's.

1949, the three new directors : Edwin Goodwin, Enoch Boulton and Alfred Tomkinson (left to right)

28

One employee, Bill Thomas, the Works Inspector and Lodgeman, lived with his family in a cottage adjacent to the factory. He had played an active part in raising the fire alert and had telephoned the directors from the offices before being driven out by the heat and smoke. He continued to provide practical help to the firm in the difficult months which followed, not least by making his front room available as a temporary boardroom.

Many offers of help were received from other pottery manufacturers, in particular the Whieldon Sanitary Co. who loaned part of their new warehouse for laying out orders and stocking wares. The factory was out of operation for five months, losing an estimated £3,000 to £4,000 per week. However, without the assistance of the other potteries, production could not have commenced for a further three months.

For a considerable time after restarting, only ground floor space was available together with some old cottages quickly converted into painting shops. Even so, output of fancies and musical jugs was back to an astonishing 75% of previous production levels and small quantities of dinner and tea wares were also being made.

Unfortunately, the relevant insurances had not been sufficiently upgraded to reflect the considerable investments made during the modernisations completed just prior to the fire. As a result, the company was under-insured which created a further burden on financial resources. Nevertheless, rebuilding continued until, by August 1956, the majority of the loss had been made good. As on previous occasions, misfortune was turned to advantage with the reconstruction incorporating many of the latest machines and ideas. These included up-to-date printing shops and warehouses together with an air-conditioned showroom. The building works were finished in the spring of 1957 to complete the pottery's resurrection.

The fire and consequent rebuilding also brought about the relocation of the associated company of C.J. Baines. A significant colour manufacturer in which the Fielding family were major shareholders, it had operated from the Sutherland Street works for many years.

During this period, Reginald was persuaded to use the services of a 'Time and Motion' consultant with the aim of increasing productivity. The review of working practices was planned to encompass the entire factory. However, by the time the study of the clay and biscuit departments had been completed, Reginald decided that the benefits achieved were insufficient to justify the continued cost and the project was abandoned.

The changes to the fabric of the factory were mirrored, inevitably, by changes in personnel. Three new directors were appointed in 1949 - Edwin Goodwin, Enoch Boulton and Alfred Tomkinson - to support Reginald as Chairman. However, the family atmosphere was retained and workers described it as a happy place to work. The prevailing community spirit can be illustrated by the Christmas parties in all departments, the annual staff outings to Mucklestone Point-to-Point Races and the trips to seaside resorts such as Bournemouth and Hastings. A memorable visit to New Brighton featured dancing on the ferry whilst, in a more serious mood, the outing to London included a guided tour of the Houses of Parliament by the local MP, Mr Ellis Smith.

Francis Edward (Ned) Taylor

Construction of new Litherland kilns alongside demolition of the old bottle kilns

Several key people were lost to the firm during the 1950's and 1960's, the first of whom was Enoch Boulton. Joining in 1929 as Chief Designer and Decorating Manager, he had been instrumental in the transformation of the product range during the 1930's. He left, in 1950, to take up the position of Commercial Director at Coalport China. The new Art Director was William Kemp.

After 40 years service as head artist, Walter Lamonby died in June 1952. He had been an outstanding pupil at the Stoke School of Art, serving his apprenticeship as a pottery painter with George Jones & Sons Ltd, and had worked for John Aynsley & Sons Ltd before joining the Devon Pottery.

The family and the firm both suffered from the loss of Francis Edward (Ned) Taylor on his death in May 1960, at the age of 69. A nephew of Abraham Fielding and a director of the firm for many years, he had been a noted sportsman as a horseman, footballer, tennis player, cricketer and cyclist. He had been educated at Hanley High School where he was athletics champion in 1907 and he began horse riding at an early age under the guidance of William Boxhall, Huntsman to the Duke of Sutherland. As a footballer, he had played league football for, amongst others, Stoke City and Port Vale Football Clubs as an amateur. In a less strenuous field, he had been a successful dog breeder and exhibitor of Terriers at Crufts. Ned had remained a bachelor and is remembered fondly today, by those who worked with him, as a 'real character'!

Two years later, in November 1962, another long-serving member of the company died. Edwin Goodwin had joined Abraham in 1901 eventually becoming the Company Secretary. He was succeeded by his deputy of many years, Arnold Kennerley, who had himself been with the firm since he joined as a junior office boy at the age of 14 in 1930.

During 1963, modernisation was again in progress with the replacement of the two bottle ovens, built in the earliest days of the pottery, with two Litherland intermittent gas-fired kilns.

Using the old bottle ovens, biscuit firing took a fortnight from the time of placing until the ware could be removed but the new kilns provided a 24 - 35 hour service. The ability to draw eight trucks a day gave a 10% increase in capacity and handling the ware became simpler with the smaller batches. The intermittent kiln provided a flexible and economical means of achieving the factory's production requirements which averaged a minimum of 2,600 dozen pieces a week at this time.

The bottle ovens remained in operation whilst the new kilns were being installed. Hence, building of the new took place alongside the gradual dismantling of the old. Interestingly, the demolition uncovered some of the original construction methods including the use of railway sleepers and iron rails as floor supports.

The general reconstruction and modernisation of production facilities during the post-war years was accompanied by a transformation of the pottery industry with a reduction in the number of smaller manufacturers, either through acquisition by larger firms or liquidation. This restructuring gathered pace from the late 1950's in the face of increased competition from overseas producers, particularly those from Japan and Germany. The prospect of joining the European Common Market in 1962 also presented a new and significant challenge to the traditional export sales philosophies. S. Fielding & Co. Ltd was one of the medium-sized companies which continued to trade successfully by combining competent management, a good reputation and market specialisation with mergers or take-overs.

However, the changing nature of the pottery industry did lead Reginald into a reappraisal of his business and to the conclusion that a new impetus was needed. As a result, part of the company was sold to Douglas Kitchener Bailey in 1963. Bailey had many business interests and had previously been a key figure at the Howard Pottery at Shelton. Reginald Fielding and Douglas Bailey became the joint Managing Directors, although with very different management styles.

One of the first effects of Bailey's influence was the re-introduction of cellulose wares, of which he had had considerable experience at the Howard Pottery. A separate company, Baifield Productions Ltd, was formed for this venture although it operated in much the same way as the Era Art Pottery had done in the 1930's. Indeed, it used one of Era's tradenames, Ranleigh Ware.

At about the same time, early 1964, Fielding's took over the rival earthenware manufacturer, Shorter and Sons Ltd. Shorter's had found themselves with significant financial problems, not least the cost of converting to smokeless firing in order to conform with the Clean Air Act. A further contributory factor was the proposed loss of part of their factory site in a road widening scheme.

Shorter and Sons Ltd had been founded in 1875 and there were many similarities between the two firms - both had had strong family involvement through several generations and both produced ornamental, tableware and novelty lines.

After the take-over, Shorter's continued to trade under their own name within the newly styled Fielding Group Potteries which also included Baifield Productions Ltd. All manufacture for the Group was centred at the Devon Pottery which was further extended to accommodate the extra production. The Group also became the sole concessionaires for Johansfors Swedish glass during this period.

Reginald was prevented from taking his usual active involvement in the day to day running of the company when, towards the end of 1965, he suffered a heart attack which resulted in an enforced stay in hospital. Although he recovered well, he obviously had to take things at a slower pace for a while. However, he always had time to uphold the family tradition of acknowledging loyal service. This was demonstrated again the following year in the presentation of a gold watch to Mrs Annie Bentley on her completion of 60 years with the company as a gold transferer.

The Fielding family connection with the company came to an end with Reginald's retirement in 1967. Douglas Bailey acquired the entire company and became Chairman of the Board of S. Fielding & Co. Ltd and each of the Group's subsidiary companies. Apart from his industrial activities, and perhaps because both his sons were doctors, Douglas Bailey took a great interest in the work of the Royal College of Surgeons. As a result of his support, he was made a member of its Court of Patrons.

Further new faces were to appear during the following years, indeed the senior personnel changed more frequently than at any previous time in the company's history. One of the new appointments was that of Stanley Barnes as Managing Director in 1970. He brought a wealth of experience of the industry having formerly been a director of Ridgway Potteries Ltd and also associated with the Alfred Clough Group for 12 years having been the sales director of W.H. Grindley & Co. Ltd immediately prior to taking up his new position.

Two significant changes to the Board of Directors occurred in the first half of 1971. With the death of Douglas Bailey in March, his wife took over the reins of the business and, with the departure of John Shorter, in July, Christopher Ward was brought into the firm as Chief Sales Executive. Another member of the W.H. Grindley & Co. Ltd team, he now became completely responsible for all sales and marketing, both home and export, for the Group.

In 1976, Mrs Bailey sold the Fielding Group of Companies to The Archibald Bathgate Group, a Liverpool based firm of accountants. However, it appears that the directors and senior staff remained in place following the change of ownership. Indeed, when Stanley Barnes retired in 1979, Mr Ward became the Chief Executive.

Ultimately, the deepening recession which had destroyed 20,000 jobs in the pottery industry took its toll. After suffering losses of nearly half a million pounds in the previous two years, the workers clocked off for the last time on December 17th 1982 and the Devon Pottery closed its gates. It was a sad day for all concerned, not only because of the problem of finding alternative employment in such difficult times, but also the loss of what many regarded as their second home and the break-up of a happy family.

The works, blocks and cases were bought from the liquidator by the Caverswall China Company Ltd early in 1983 who transferred their mould making and printing departments to the Devon Pottery site. However, Caverswall soon ran into problems themselves which resulted in their acquisition, in 1984/85, by Thomas Goode and Company, a retailer of high quality ceramics, glass and luxury goods.

The Caverswall China Company was subsequently offered for sale as a going concern and was purchased by Bullers PLC in 1986. A year later, thousands of Crown Devon and Shorter blocks and case moulds were sold by public auction. Following the three day sale, the works were demolished.

Abraham Fielding in 1919

The Growth of a Business

The policy of diversity; exhibitions, marketing and promotional
activities

There were several key features of the firm's approach which contributed to the success and growth of the business. Their creativity and diversity of production, which few other firms could match, meant that they were able to meet the demands of changing trends while appealing to a broader based market. Their competitive attitude toward home and overseas markets was exemplified by extensive promotional activities, often personally supported by senior staff. However, probably the most important factor was that their policies were founded on providing good quality products at competitive prices, something that the English pottery industry regularly failed to do.

Establishing a Reputation

Hackney, Kirkham & Co, the firm in which Simon Fielding had invested, were producers of majolica, jasper, jet, Rockingham, Vigonian, green-glaze goods, toilet ware and some fancy goods. For a small pottery, the range of articles was wide and varied encompassing dessert, tea and beer sets as well as dental spittoons, garden seats and tiles. Through the association with the Fielding colour mill, they were able to directly benefit from the innovations in glaze and colour being made by Abraham. This was demonstrated, in 1879, when they launched a new product on which the Pottery Gazette reported :

> *Messrs F. Hackney & Co of Stoke have recently been manufacturing some new umbrella stands. They are in the new Argenta ware which is the nearest imitation to the colour of silver that can be produced in potting. The design is rustic representing the stump of a tree.*

After his take-over of the pottery, Abraham initially continued with the same product lines. The range of shapes and patterns was progressively extended with particular emphasis being placed on the majolica goods which achieved considerable success.

The firm increasingly benefited from Abraham's influence and, not least, his ability to keep pace with or indeed foresee the changes in market taste. He realised that the manufacture of fancy goods was being neglected by the English potters due to the predominance of cheap foreign imports. In later years, Abraham would relate how he was prompted to take on the competition. Passing a Longton shop window, he noticed a decorated bread tray priced at 1s 6d. He bought the item and confirmed that it was of German manufacture as he had expected. He decided that he could make such articles as the bread tray as well as sardine boxes, butter dishes and biscuit jars to retail at the same price as the imported items and yet yield him a fair profit. To put this decision into perspective, an English made biscuit jar could not be purchased for less than about 7s 6d at this time. It is not surprising, therefore, that when Abraham put one on the market at one shilling, people seriously questioned his sanity!

His next step was to visit the Leipzig Fair to see first-hand what the Germans were producing. He bought three packages of goods at the fair and, from an examination of them, he decided on his future course of action. He set a staff of modellers to work, not copying the German wares but using them as a guide. As a result, a range of fancy table lines in pottery evolved which were to sell powerfully for many years and lead to significant development of the factory. Hence, with the decline in the appeal of

Advertisement from the Pottery Gazette, 1897, illustrating a selection of useful and ornamental wares. The china teaware is particularly interesting.

majolica, the firm was ready with their new productions in art vases, flowerpots and similar items as well as expanding their noted strengths for toilet and dinner wares.

An aggressive approach to pricing was adopted and fully supported by extensive advertising. This was shown in the competitive stance taken by Abraham against cheap foreign goods and it continued to be a major sales tenet for many years. The Pottery Gazette summed up the Fielding attitude, rather poetically, in January 1894 :

> .... they believing in a quantity of nimble shillings before the lonely slow sovereign

Equally important, a plan for improving quality was also set in place. This was demonstrated, in 1895, by the decision to enhance the decorations by using scoured gold instead of the ordinary (and cheaper) liquid gold used previously. The change was made without any increase in price. At the same time, the unusual step was taken of guaranteeing all wares against crazing which was a prevalent problem.

The policy of quality improvement coupled with a constant flow of new patterns and shapes at prices which ensured a quick turn-over by the retailers combined to rapidly establish the reputation of the firm as an important earthenware manufacturer.

By 1896, it was necessary to move their London showrooms to larger premises at Ely Place, Holborn. This enabled Fielding's to show effectively a representative sample of their range of wares which had grown to encompass all types of useful and ornamental items. The range included vases, pedestals, baskets, luncheon trays, biscuit trays, honey jars, fruit dishes and trays, jug sets, cheese stands and covers, egg frames, teapots, dinner and tea wares.

To coincide with this expansion, a new price list was published which was praised for being one of the best illustrated available to the public. A further indication of a growing confidence was the offer to send goods on approval to prospective customers and to bear all the cost of return if they were not satisfactory.

Apart from the consistent freshness of their ideas in form and ornamentation, a number of other factors typified Fielding's products and approach. One was their use of colour and the care taken in design and manufacture. This was highlighted in a Pottery Gazette report of August 1901 :

> The firm does not profess to make the most expensive type of decorated pottery, but on the other hand, they do not make anything that is in bad taste or carelessly produced.

A further feature was the application of a decoration to a complete range of articles, from a sardine box through to a vase and pedestal, to form a suite of matching wares. Finally, as has been noted, they aimed at supplying popular products at reasonable prices. This philosophy was re-inforced by advertisements which exhorted retailers to handle the attractive lines which they supplied as a remedy for the bad trading conditions of the time. They also offered to supply a sample £10 crate on approval to buyers in towns not represented as an added incentive.

View of the warehouse at the Devon Pottery in 1914

View of the showroom at the Devon Pottery in 1914

Their overall approach was obviously successful since before long new advertisements were being issued. These comprised two full pages and declared that the company was determined to continue its lead in the introduction of new shapes and styles despite the attempts to imitate them by several manufacturers. However, they did discontinue the issue of catalogues!

Energy and Enterprise

By 1905, the company was well-established as an earthenware manufacturer producing high quality goods at reasonable prices for the middle class trade. Noted for their wide range of products, they were described in the Pottery Gazette as :

> .... *full of energy and enterprise. Season after season they place novelties on the market with unfailing regularity.*

Increasing popularity and consequent expansion of the business resulted in two moves of London showrooms in as many years, each of which provided greater display areas. In 1908, the break was made with Mr Charles Berry, who had represented the company in London since 1896, when the showrooms were moved from his premises at Ely Place to Gamage Buildings, Holborn Circus where Mr C.J. Pratt acted as the representative. The showrooms were moved again in late 1909 but this time only to a different floor within the same building. The representative was now Mr Hooper who had considerable experience in the retail trade and whose sound advice was to prove of significant benefit.

One aspect of business in which Fielding's showed particular initiative was in providing different pieces and presentation sets each year specially for the Christmas trade. In 1905, these included match strikers in quaint shapes, small ashtrays and numerous miniature lines. Indeed, miniatures became a regular feature since they had the dual advantage of providing an acceptable gift which might also encourage an interest in the larger articles. For 1910, clock cases, bulb bowls and dainty afternoon sets were offered. The bulb bowls catered for the increasing popularity of home grown bulbs whilst modelling them so that they could be used as salad bowls or flower holders during the summer months. The afternoon sets were presented on a tray, described as 'Kaynoak', the tray bottom being of oak and the sides of canework.

The company consistently pursued orders in both the home and export markets, using a variety of promotional activities to bring their wares to the attention of the retail trade and buying public. Exhibitions were a particularly useful method of reaching a wide audience. It is not surprising, therefore, that they participated strongly in a series of such events held from 1915 onwards.

Against a backdrop of the First World War, the first British Industries Fair was held in May 1915 at the Agricultural Hall, Islington. It was organised by the Board of Trade with the object of putting British manufacturers in touch with buyers who had previously purchased primarily from the 'enemy' (sic) countries of Germany and Austria. In an attempt to emulate the large continental trade fairs, such as the ones held at Leipzig, the event provided a showcase for some 620 firms in five trade sections. In spite of the various difficulties being experienced by the pottery manufacturers,

Original drawings of tile designs, date unknown

Two selections of vellum wares. Patterns in the lower photograph include Pendant, Thames, Eva, Etna and Dora (top, left to right) with Elm, Erin and Wick (bottom, left to right).

Early wares including examples of the popular Pearline (teapot, bottom right), Silverine (teapot, bottom centre) and Indian (dish, top right).

Various en-suite wares decorated with the Royal Devon pattern

Advertisement from the Pottery Gazette, 1895, for Royal Clarence

Royal Delft

Examples of the artist's work. The coffee cups to the foreground were decorated by Walter Lamonby on Tuscan china whiteware.

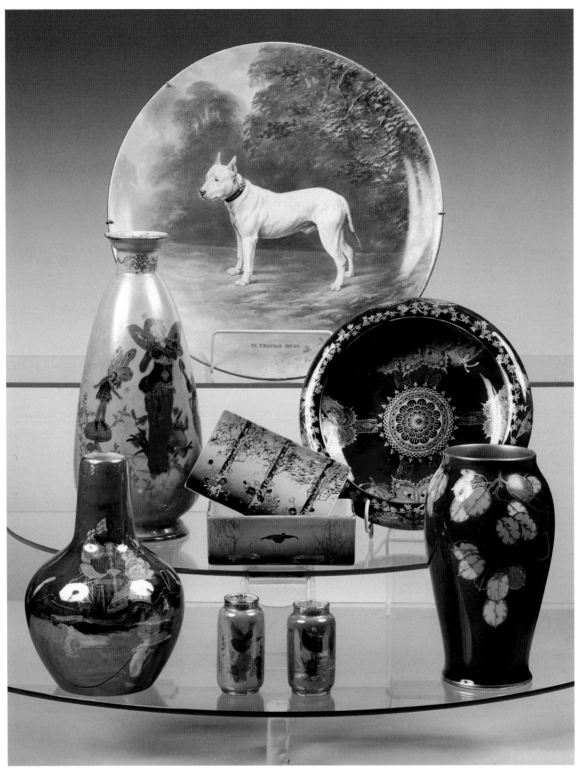

Lustrine patterns including Sylvan Butterflies (bowl, centre right), Royal George (vase, bottom left) and Birch (cigarette box, centre)

not least the shortage of labour, the Pottery and Glass Section was well-supported. Fielding's took advantage of the event to show a typical range of their wares, particularly vases and table fancies, re-inforcing their reputation as suppliers of quality goods with popular appeal.

The following year, the British Industries Fair moved to the Victoria and Albert Museum and attracted buyers from throughout the world. However, the new location was not an overwhelming success with complaints being made about the lack of space and privacy whilst the Pottery Gazette commented that :

> It would certainly be an improvement if the exhibition could be held in future in premises wherein there are freer facilities for transacting business in the normal way; for instance, it was an infliction, no doubt, upon a good many of the overseas buyers that they were not permitted to smoke their customary cigars whilst negotiating their business.

Surmounting these difficulties, Fielding's showed a full complement of useful table articles and an almost limitless variety of ornaments to advantage.

Held at the same venue in 1917, many of the problems persisted. However, the event was becoming well-established with increases in both the number of exhibitors and visitors over the previous year. A further seal of approval was gained by the attendance of several members of the royal family, in particular the Queen who made a number of purchases. The company had secured a spacious stand in a good corner position where they mounted an impressive display of their products. Whilst their noted strengths in toilet, dinner and table wares were well represented, it was the selection of large ornamental pieces which stole the limelight bringing justified praise.

For the next two years, the British Industries Fair moved to a warehouse in the London Docks where conditions also left a lot to be desired. In general, the pottery manufacturers continued to have difficulty in meeting orders because of wartime restrictions and their aftermath. However, demand was growing albeit from a changing marketplace, highlighted by the Pottery Gazette in a rather tactless manner :

> .... the changed social conditions of the present time, the more cultured classes being poorer, whilst the less educated sections of the community have plenty of money to spend.

Abraham's response to such elitist comments is a matter for interesting speculation since it was his philosophy to bring good design within the reach of all levels of society.

In both years, large stands provided Fielding's with the opportunity of showing an interesting cross-section of their products. As on previous occasions, existing popular ranges were displayed often with new variations whilst completely new wares were also launched.

The British Industries Fair came of age in 1920 with its move to the Crystal Palace which finally offered exhibitors the space and facilities they required. However, continuing

Advertisement from the Pottery Gazette, 1917, emphasising the ornamental ranges including the artist's work which is also illustrated on framed wall plaques.

production and trading difficulties resulted in an inability of most manufacturers to meet the increasing demand, particularly from the home market. Everyday utilitarian articles together with dinner and tea wares were much sought after by the visiting trade buyers. In contrast to these requirements, many potteries had mounted elaborate displays of highly ornamental goods. The Devon Pottery achieved a balance to their stand, showing a combination of domestic tableware and toilet sets alongside a large variety of more ornamental articles including a new series of figures.

The British Institute of Industrial Art mounted its first Exhibition of Modern Art in Knightsbridge during the summer of 1920. The dual aims of the Institute were to stimulate art in industry and to improve the standard of public taste by bringing adjudicated work prominently forward. Hence, all wares submitted by the exhibitors had to satisfy the selection committee. This factor, together with the limited preparation time available, may have contributed to the lack of support from the manufacturers. However, those that did participate received considerable praise from the trade press, typified by the following report in the Pottery Gazette :

> *Their contributions to the British Industrial Art Exhibition have been made with a larger and wider view - that of personal prestige on the one hand, and the support and encouragement of a worthy ideal on the other. Those manufacturers who have taken the trouble to be represented in this first exhibition are to be congratulated on their broad and imperialistic vision. Their actual recompense for taking part in such an effort is likely to be abstract rather than direct, but the abstract things are, nevertheless, sometimes very real, and, cumulative also.*

Needless to say, Abraham adopted the larger and wider view submitting an exhibit of practical everyday earthenware which demonstrated fully the firm's ability to supply well-designed articles which achieved an imposing effect at a moderate price.

By 1921, the economic climate had changed with a shortage of orders creating a highly competitive atmosphere at the British Industries Fair. Fielding's met the challenge with a comprehensive display of toiletware and a variety of useful and ornamental products. The vellum ground ranges, on which their reputation had been consolidated, were on view in a number of new decorative styles and in almost every conceivable domestic article. In addition, lustre, figure and handpainted wares demonstrated the enormous scope of the company.

During the mid-1920's, the energy and enterprise of the Devon Pottery was undiminished. Longstanding popular product lines were regularly augmented with new ranges thereby ensuring a high level of exposure in the trade press and cordial relationships with the retail buyers. In a prophetic report in 1924, the Pottery Gazette stated :

> *The wonderful variety that is to be seen in the productions of this house is one of the talks of the trade, and the way in which many unique styles of decoration have been popularised at the Devon Pottery, and brought within the reach of people of ordinary means, is something that will, no doubt, live on beyond our time.*

View of the British Industries Fair at Crystal Palace, 1920

The British Empire Exhibition held at Wembley in 1924 was perhaps the largest event of its kind to have been held worldwide. Covering some 216 acres, it was described as the world's biggest shop window. The Pottery and Glass Section was housed in the Palace of Industry and provided an impressive display. However, the number of potteries participating was not as great as might have been expected for such a prestigious event. In common with the other firms taking part, Fielding's produced new lines specifically for the exhibition, most notably a series of lustre floating bowls, as well as showing the best of their regular ranges.

By 1926, the 'Buy British Goods Campaign' was well underway and this, together with financial assistance from the Board of Trade and vocal support from the royal family, contributed to the success of the British Industries Fair that year. Held at the White City, Shepherds Bush, the fair attracted a considerable number of visitors from overseas as well as trade buyers from throughout the UK. As in previous years, the Fielding stand had a good display typical of its wide range of production. The stand was further enhanced by a selection of pieces in rich lustred flambe effects featuring painted and gilt patterns.

The same year, the Potteries promoted themselves by holding a Civic Week, in May, with the object of directing attention to the importance of the area as an industrial and commercial centre. Amongst other attractions, an exhibition of modern pottery was held in the King's Hall, Stoke-on-Trent whilst a number of factories were open for inspection. The Fielding company was fully involved in these activities, both participating in the exhibition and opening the Devon Pottery to visitors. Unfortunately, the entire enterprise was overshadowed by the General Strike, the resultant transport difficulties reducing its impact to that of a local show.

In a new departure, the British Industries Fair in 1929 allowed the general public to attend, from 4 pm until 8 pm each day, in the expectation that this would create a wider interest in the newest goods being produced. There was certainly plenty to see on the Fielding stand which provided unmistakable evidence of their considerable design activity in the preceding months. The solid requirements for tableware were, as always, well catered for. However, in addition, a wealth of individual articles and small services suitable as presents were offered. These included dessert and salad sets, coffee and early morning sets on wicker trays, and every conceivable form of table 'extra'. The Pottery Gazette remarked :

> *It almost seemed as though the firm has embarked upon a new era and, strangely enough, they have a new Era shape in tableware modelled throughout.*

Also featured was a limited number of pieces of studio pottery produced by Mr Lewis Neaverson. A well-known china dealer based in Huddersfield, he had experimented with blended glaze effects in his own studio where he had conducted special firings in a small electric kiln. Unfortunately, no further information is available and the success of this venture is unknown.

The new decade started with considerable uncertainty due to the ever deepening economic recession. The company's answer to an increasingly competitive market was one of creativity, innovation and expansion but certainly not retreat. Building on the design activity of the previous two years, the campaign for new shapes and decorations was dramatically extended at considerable expense. In such adverse trading conditions, the company's team spirit, fostered over many years, provided the bedrock for this approach. In recognising the determination being shown, the Pottery Gazette commented :

> *It would appear that every member of the firm has been specially exerting himself in a 'long, strong pull, altogether' aiming at making Crown Devon ware even more popular in the trade than it has formerly been; and one must not regard the former reputation of Crown Devon too glibly.*

The British Industries Fair of 1931, held at Olympia, reflected the prevalent difficulties with the withdrawal of several important potteries. Characteristically, against this background, Fielding's presented a display described as one of the best of the whole fair. A particular feature was their new line, called 'Checks'. However, the crowning glory of the stand was the extensive range of novelty wares.

The export drive was boosted, in 1931, by the British Empire Trade Exhibition held in Buenos Aires. Crown Devon ware was exhibited in unique surroundings and drew large groups of interested visitors.

The depression continued to exact its toll and the British Industries Fairs of 1932 and 1933 were sombre events, poorly supported by a significant number of the major manufacturers. This was seen to be particularly disappointing when great efforts were being made generally to reinfuse life and vigour into British industry. Fielding's followed their established pattern of showing a good variety of wares, from popularly priced to relatively expensive, encompassing proven best-sellers and new ranges.

By 1934, a more optimistic mood prevailed in the industry. Throughout the period, the company had maintained its high level of popularity by consistently updating their product ranges and actively pursuing business at home and abroad. Although the main on-going sales impetus had been through the London showrooms and the travelling representatives, visitors to the factory had always been encouraged. This aspect was further enhanced, in 1934, by the provision of a new showroom at the factory. Hence, visitors no longer needed to make a tour of the warehouses and workshops in order to see the latest creations. The showroom was of a simple yet modern design with fixtures finished in a matt textured plastic, giving the impression of stone, which allowed the pottery to be shown to best effect.

The British Industries Fairs of 1935 and 1936 were larger and more representative of the industry generally than had been the case for several years. More trade buyers attended and a greater demand for better quality goods was noted. By means of a display which ranged from useful tableware to an exceptional array of novelty items, Fielding's made a strong bid to capture the interest of these trade buyers. They were justifiably successful and reported good business in all departments.

Two views of the new showroom at the Devon pottery, 1934

S. Fielding & Co stand at the British Industries Fair, 1930's

Part of the display at the British Industries Fair, 1932, featuring the Mattajade range.

Matt black vellum grounds including the patterns Mavis (ginger jar, top and plate, centre), Daisy (bottom centre), Chelsea (vases, bottom left and right) and Wye (vases, centre left and right)

Era shaped tablewares

A selection of hand painted jugs decorated with the typical stylised floral designs of the late 1920's and the 1930's.

Advertising postcard, 1930's.

1930's tablewares including Cunard cube teapots.

Bold geometric and floral designs shown on a range of tablewares.

AS SUPPLIED TO H.M. QUEEN MARY AND H.H. DUCHESS OF YORK.

Advertising leaflet for the Checks pattern showing the availability of co-ordinated table linen.

Examples of hand painted tablewares including Modane shape coffee cups (bottom) and a Vogue shape gravy boat (centre right).

Hand painted ornamental wares from the 1930's.

Display stands provided to retailers for special displays of figures and musical novelties, 1937.

The provision of sales aids to retailers engendered cordial relations and encouraged them to give prominence to displays of Crown Devon. In time for the Christmas trade of 1936, two special window stands were devised, for figures and musical novelties respectively. Available on loan to the shops, the stands were constructed of three-ply and had chromium pillars and alcoves. Fully fitted for electric illumination, they were supplied ready to use. The offer was taken up enthusiastically with every available stand in use and a high level of sales reported as a result. Such assistance was not restricted to the home market, variations of the display material being utilised by major stockists throughout the world.

The unsettled political situation kept the buyers away from the British Industries Fair of 1938. With hindsight, the comments expressed in the Pottery Gazette report of the fair are chillingly pathetic :

> *Let us hope that, by the time next year's Fair comes round, the European situation will have become easier, all rumours of the possibilities of war ruled out, and trade conditions, as a result, rendered more normal.*

Of course, nothing could have been further from the truth and, although business held up reasonably well given the circumstances, 1939 was not a record-breaking sales year for any manufacturer. However, against this background of upheaval and uncertainty, Fielding's continued to introduce new designs and, therefore, were well poised for the export drive to come.

Concentration on Exports

As in many other sectors, war-time conditions caused the government to become increasingly involved in all aspects of the pottery industry. Although often acting for the best motives of national interest, the result was invariably to make life more difficult for the manufacturers.

The first of a series of regulations came into force under the Prices and Goods Act of 1940 which sought to restrict prices and profit margins to those customary before the war. The object was to prevent profiteering and the penalties for infringement were severe. This was soon followed by the Limitation of Supplies (Misc) Order which limited supplies of pottery and glassware to retailers to two-thirds of the value of supplies received in the six months ending November 30th 1939.

This quota system was designed to prevent labour being used for home trade production when it could be deployed for export trade or munitions working. However, many manufacturers were badly affected by it, being compelled to suspend large numbers of workers in spite of having plenty of orders on their books. Many firms had to face the possibility of closing down for the duration of the war.

By May 1941, the Board of Trade had recognised the problems and prepared a scheme for the concentration of the pottery industry, winning acceptance for it from the British Pottery Manufacturers' Federation. The aims of the scheme were to release labour for munitions, provide storage accommodation, preserve as far as possible the export trade and to concentrate production in as few factories as possible so that those factories remaining in business worked to full capacity.

In most cases, this meant that a firm had to take over the production of another factory in order to qualify. However, the nucleus firms then had an obligation to keep intact the premises and plant of the business which they had taken over and closed down. Certain advantages and protection was afforded to the nucleus companies including their inclusion on the list of protected firms which resulted in a lower age of reservation for their workers. They also received preferential treatment in relation to government orders, supplies of raw materials were safeguarded as far as possible and their factories would not be requisitioned. Workers right of employment and pay were also safeguarded. S. Fielding & Co. Ltd were one of the first to apply and be granted a nucleus certificate, taking over Shore & Coggins in order to assist their qualification.

A year later, in a further effort to alleviate the shortage of utility wares, the Board of Trade withdrew the home trade quota for decorated wares and the quota-free concessions in respect of coloured bodies and glazes. As a counter-balance, pottery for the home market was made entirely quota-free. However, apart from export rejects, it was restricted to the plain white or ivory articles which had enjoyed exemption for the preceding six months. Production was limited to teacups and saucers, breakfast cups and saucers, mugs, beakers, plates, coffee pots, teapots, jugs, sauce boats, meat dishes, vegetable dishes, casseroles, pie dishes, bowls, basins, ewers and chambers. The manufacture of all other items of domestic pottery and art pottery was forbidden from June 1st 1942.

Together with restricting the type of ware that could be produced, by the Domestic Pottery (Manufacture & Supply) Order, prices charged at all stages of distribution from the manufacturer to the general public were also controlled by the Domestic Pottery (Maximum Prices) Order. Manufacturers, licensed by the Board of Trade under these orders, were classified into three groups according to the maximum prices that could be charged for their ware having regard for their costs of production. All wares had to be marked with a letter indicating to which group it belonged; Group I articles were identified by the letter 'C', Group II by the letter 'B' and Group III by the letter 'A'. Fielding's were licenced as a Group III manufacturer.

Regulations were also imposed in relation to export goods. With the exception of South America, the USA and Canada, the supply of decorated wares was initially restricted on a quota system. However, in August 1942, a total ban was imposed although the Americas were again excluded. By this action, it was estimated that over half the decorators remaining in the industry could be released either for the Services or for work in munitions and other essential industries.

Whilst the export trade constraints were lifted after the end of the war, decorated pottery could not be manufactured specifically for the home market again until May 1952. Hence, sales and marketing energies were directed predominantly towards overseas buyers in the immediate post-war period.

Fielding's had always maintained a well-balanced approach to the home and export markets. They had regularly attended promotional exhibitions overseas and were represented

Two advertisements from the Pottery Gazette of 1942 (top) and 1944 (bottom)

by established agents in a number of countries. These activities had been supported by regular visits from senior personnel, particularly Reg Fielding.

During the war, they continued to export to the best of their ability, given the various government restrictions, and had particular success in the South American countries. The late Forties witnessed their participation in an increasing number of overseas events, either in their own right or under the auspices of their agents. This flexible attitude is demonstrated by two events in 1948. In March, the Annual Agriculture and Industrial Fair (known as the Rand Show) held in Johannesburg featured Crown Devon wares as part of the composite display of McLaren Campbell & Co. Their excellent stand won the 'Buy Empire Goods' Perpetual Challenge Trophy for the best, most complete and most attractive exhibit of goods made within the British Commonwealth. September saw Fielding's taking part in the British Exhibition in Copenhagen which was the most comprehensive display of British goods ever staged in Scandinavia. The exhibits won high praise drawing a large and enthusiastic attendance of buyers from all over Scandinavia and Europe.

Further agents were progressively recruited so that, by 1950, the company had representatives not only in their traditional markets of Australia, Canada, America, New Zealand, South Africa and South America but also in Switzerland, Belgium, Italy, Costa Rica and Malta. In addition, a specialist London agent handled their business in the Far East including Hong Kong, Singapore and Malaya.

At home, the British Industries Fair was re-instated, in 1947, after its war time suspension. However, it was not well supported by the pottery manufacturers and never regained its pre-war prominence. It was to be replaced by the Harrogate Gifts and Fancy Goods Fair as the premier marketing vehicle for the pottery industry. However, the Harrogate fair was far from ideal with many exhibitors suffering from a lack of suitable space for their displays. It was also spread between several hotels adding to the inconvenience of visiting buyers although a free taxi link service was provided.

The increasing pressure on space resulted in the fair being moved to Blackpool in 1956. Again, the arrangements were less than satisfactory with the lighting and fitting facilities attracting particular criticism. Indeed, Reg was prompted to write to the Pottery and Glass Record after the fair expressing his dissatisfaction and highlighting the lack of foresight of the organisers in their allocation of all the work to just one contractor.

Standards did steadily improve, the fair recording an increasing number of exhibitors and visitors for each year of the Fifties and early Sixties. However, split sites and lack of space continued to create problems causing the trade press to comment that the fair was sprawling and amateurish in comparison to the continental fairs.

Drawing together, as it did, the majority of manufacturers, the fair did reflect the changing and prevailing market conditions each year. For example, 1957 saw an accent on bright colours and a swing to fancy tablewares by a number of companies. Obviously, this increased the competition for the traditional producers of these wares such as Crown Devon. However, their years of experience stood the firm in good stead enabling them to stay ahead and maintain their prominent position. The range of overseas buyers also fluctuated from year to year with a large number of Canadian

Oscar Hornsleth's stand, featuring Crown Devon, at the British Exhibition in Copenhagen, 1948.

Crown Devon's South African agent, Mr Frysh, in the Johannesburg showroom, 1956.

View of the new showroom at the Devon Pottery, 1956. The shelves were faced with oak, the room was air-conditioned and the door air-tight keeping the problem of dust to a minimum.

Reginald with the London agent, Vernon Soleil, at the London showrooms, 1964.

buyers attending in 1958 whilst there was a predominance of European visitors the following year.

Fielding's usually featured new product ranges each year in addition to their best selling established designs. Favourable reports were often received from the trade press, with particular mention being made of their colourful and interesting displays. In 1960, the Pottery Gazette also commented that :

> *S. Fielding & Co. Ltd can usually be reckoned to produce something outstanding in the way of novelty and fancy tableware.*

Given the highly competitive atmosphere of these events, almost any advantage that could be gained was to be welcomed. Hence, in 1962, the company was pleased to enjoy the 'bonus' of having their stand located in close proximity to the lift and tea bars!

Other marketing and promotional opportunities were not ignored, for example the Pottery Week held in Nottingham in April 1960. Fielding's arranged for one of their paintress' to give demonstrations during the week at Pearson's department store.

The prospect of joining the European Common Market in 1962 focussed the attention of the whole pottery industry. Whilst it offered the opportunity of increased trade with Europe, it also threatened severe competition from the continental manufacturers in the home market. British potteries responded with a promise of keen prices, good deliveries and guaranteed replacements. The collapse of the negotiations caused some uncertainty at the Blackpool Fair of 1963 but any adverse effect was minimal.

The mid to late Sixties saw a continuation of the marketing strategy including annual attendance at Blackpool together with appearances at selected overseas exhibitions. Perhaps most notable was the firm's participation in 1965 and 1967 in the Paris Tableware Salon held at the Parc des Expositions. This was a distinguished and elegant show mainly attended by French manufacturers. For Fielding's, it provided an excellent opportunity for meeting buyers from all over Europe.

Perhaps the most notable feature of marketing policy in the 1970's was the decision to stop advertising in the trade press. Advertising had long been an essential component of the company's strategy with regular advertisements of at least a half-page being placed, particularly to highlight new designs and product ranges. However, this stopped dramatically and, from January 1972, virtually no advertisements appeared.

Co-incidentally, reports on the company by the correspondents of the trade press also declined during this period with other manufacturers receiving the attention once lavished on Crown Devon.

Fielding's continued to exhibit at the Blackpool fair and its successor (from 1976), the International Spring Fair held at the National Exhibition Centre near Birmingham. Although these shows remained the vehicle for launching new ranges, the company was given little recognition in the reports of the events.

Crown Devon gives that keynote of individuality which makes an instant
appeal to lovers of pottery who desire dignity of design at moderate cost.

1930's advertising leaflet illustrating a selection of matt glazed wares.

Tubelined patterns including Cretian (top right) and two examples of the Dutch inspired designs, Delph (jug, centre right and miniature, top centre)

Examples of the extensive range of wall plaques available in the 1930's

A selection of matt glazed wares. The musical jug (top left) and the ornamental miniatures (bottom) are particularly interesting.

Mattita wares showing the diversity of decorating techniques utilised including flat brushwork, tubelining and embossed details.

Two selections of matt glazed, enamelled decorations, finished in gold.

Mattajade ornamental wares including Fairy Castles (jug, top right and bowl, centre right) and Chinese Dragon (vase, bottom centre).

Matt glazed enamel decorations including Parrot and Cloud (bookend, top left) and Chinese Dragon (vase, top centre).

A Diversity of Design

A description of the wares produced

The production of S. Fielding & Co was wide ranging and encompassed ornamental, toilet and table wares, novelties and gifts, advertising and commemoratives.

It has long been recognised that any company is ultimately only as good as the skill and creativity of its staff. Hence, a significant factor in Fielding's success was their ability to attract high quality people and to create an atmosphere which engendered their subsequent loyalty. Sales staff, designers, modellers and decorators combined their talents to produce a succession of innovative and extremely popular ranges which consistently confirmed the firm's position as a premier earthenware manufacturer.

Another notable aspect of the firm's approach was the provision of decorations 'en-suite'. This enabled customers to purchase a complete range of matching items, from an ashtray to a large flowerpot and pedestal, together with table and toilet wares. Obviously, the composition of these ranges varied at different times reflecting the changing social conditions. For example, the demand for toilet wares was diminishing from the 1920's onwards and, therefore, were gradually phased out.

Each shape had identifiable design characteristics, such as the position and type of embossments or the contour of the handles, and these were reflected in the various articles within the range. Consequently, a co-ordination in both form and decoration could be provided. However, it must be remembered that one shape would generally be used for many different decorations during its lifetime. Similarly, a particular pattern could be applied to several different shapes resulting in a further aspect of the en-suite principle, i.e. a matching decoration on items from various shape ranges.

Although a significant marketing policy, the en-suite approach did not preclude the design of shapes and patterns specifically for one class of ware. Many decorations were only applied to table or toilet wares whilst the speciality ranges such as novelties and commemoratives had their own very distinctive and separate designs.

Turning The Century (1878 - 1916)

The earliest wares produced by Fielding's were a direct continuation of the product lines of F. Hackney & Co. These included **majolica**, Jet, Rockingham, terra-cotta and green-glazed goods, of which majolica was the most successful. However, the high priority given to the development of general earthenware by Abraham Fielding quickly led to significant increases in production.

Hence, as tastes changed, so majolica was phased out to be replaced primarily by vellum and ivory based decorations. This style was to stand the firm in good stead for over three decades during which time, a considerable number of patterns were introduced. Predominately floral, inspiration was drawn from a variety of design sources including the Far East as demonstrated in patterns such as JAP, PEKIN and NANKIN. Such ranges competed successfully with cheap foreign imports, providing good quality for modest prices. The series of designs, collectively known as the **Royals** is perhaps the best known today. However, there were many others from the inexpensive, based on lithographic transfers, to the more elaborate involving handpainting and gilt ornamentation.

Tablewares reflected this trend with the introduction of a growing number of decorations incorporating printed or coloured under-glaze patterns. A typical example is the BOTANIC series of 1884 in which each item of dinnerware was decorated with a distinct and separate floral sketch. The important dinnerware ranges introduced at the end of the nineteenth century include OSBORNE (1891), TRENT (1894) and ELGIN (1895) which were decorated predominately with border patterns albeit in a variety of styles.

Tablewares also formed an integral and important part of the many en-suite ranges. One of the earliest was the FLUTED shape which was very popular between approximately 1886 and 1891, particularly when decorated with the OLD DERBY or INDIAN pattern. However, the LOUIS shape introduced in 1893 was perhaps the most successful, retaining its appeal for many years.

Although in the majority, flowers were not the only decorative motif used. Lithographic transfers provided the media for patterns depicting such varied subjects as Shakespeare characters, Dutch figures, landscape views and playing card suits. Similarly, vellum was not the only background colour. Indeed, colour and glaze were both used to good effect as in the flow-blue patterns and the **Pearline** range.

Careful attention was paid to the design of new shapes to complement the applied decorations. These often included features that attracted notice, as in the Pottery Gazette report of 1884 :

> *The shape of the plate is an improvement upon the old style, the edge being curved to hold the mustard and salt.*

The regular introduction of new shapes in all areas is particularly noteworthy when the inherent costs of modelling and mould making are taken into consideration. However, the same shape could be made to look totally different depending upon the patterns used and, in this way, a further level of variety and choice was made available.

Dinnerware was given a further boost in 1902 when a white body was introduced. This met the demand for a fresher, more attractive background which created the effect of a high quality product, even for the cheaper decorations.

Fielding's were aware of such trends in popular taste and, in many cases, set the benchmark for other pottery manufacturers. However, they were not afraid to buck the prevailing trend from time to time. This is particularly illustrated by the introduction of YE OLDE ENGLISH WARE in 1903 and, to a lesser extent, the SOLEILIAN series the following year.

Ye Olde English Ware aimed to appeal to those nostalgic for an earlier ceramic style and although some new shapes were used, the ornamentation was the key design element. Two main pattern subjects were involved; the first was a large red rose with green leaves whilst the second featured nicely painted fowl. The designs were completed by coloured bands and green edges to the articles. The decorations were brightly coloured although no gilding or gilt was used as it was considered that these would destroy the character of the designs.

Ye Olde English ware, 1903

Soleilian ware, 1904.

84

A report in the Pottery Gazette of February 1903 commented :

The barn fowl are absolutely novel as decorations today - though they are but reproductions of the favourites of days long past. They would appeal to those who now want a pleasing variation to the 'new art'. These birds and roses are about as complete a contrast to l'art nouveau as anything could be.

The decorations were applied to a wide range of wares including teapots, vases, flowerpots and jugs.

The Soleilian series of 1904 depicted a variety of rustic subjects of an agricultural character and was available on many useful and ornamental articles. The scenes included, in the foreground, cattle, a mare and foal, a plough, saddle and cart horses. In each case, the subjects were set against attractive scenery incorporating farm buildings whilst the whole compositions were enlivened by well-executed sunset effects which gave the series its name. This is the first known range where particular artists were attributed to designs, the two identified to date being Lucas and Debray. Items produced included a number of vases and other fancies with plain surfaces whilst the patterns showed to best effect on tall vases, ewers and jugs.

The late Victorian preference for elaborate ornamentation continued for several years and many shapes incorporated embossed details as a consequence. However, there was a gradual shift towards simpler forms with plain surfaces. This change of emphasis was seen in the new dinnerware ranges of 1909 such as QUEEN, ELY and ROYAL which were decorated with classically inspired patterns including ADAM, CECIL and CARLTON. Interestingly, the Queen shape presentation set of teapot with stand and matching hot water jug, continued to have embossments. The demand for a more delicate product was also reflected in the introduction of a hard-fired semi-porcelain body at this time. Alongside the developments in dinnerwares was a corresponding expansion in the variety and quality of general tablewares, new lines being introduced every year. Undoubtedly, the most important new decoration was the **Silverine** series. Introduced in 1910, this was to sell consistently for over forty years.

By 1911, with their established markets progressing successfully, attention was focused on the development of a better class of decorations. These employed and promoted the talents of the company's **artists** on a greater scale. The choice of subjects, for example highland cattle, seems to indicate a policy of direct competition (if not plagiarism) with factories such as Royal Worcester. The similarity did not escape the attention of the press, the ranges being described by the Daily Mail in 1914 as :

A translation into earthenware of the rich ornamentation and beautifully toned body of one of the best periods of Worcester China which has been adapted to domestic purposes as well as to a fine series of vases and other ornamental pieces.

Time of Transition (1917 - 1929)

The company continued to regularly attract praise for its ingenuity of design and responsiveness to market conditions. This is demonstrated by the following report in the Pottery Gazette of November 1917 :

> *They have a happy knack even while dealing with huge masses of ware, of always supplying some distinctive touch which imparts the quality of originality and avoids the bane of hackneyed repetition and the familiarity which breeds contempt. As an instance of this I noted a new size in cheese dishes adapted to meet the present conditions of reduced domestic rations, so that the small provision now available may not be made to appear ridiculous by being placed on a disproportionately large dish.*

A new line of black bodied vases and bowls was also introduced in 1917 which were a distinctive contrast to the majority of the ranges previously produced. The CEDRIC pattern comprised an upper part of mauve roses at regular intervals on a yellow ground whilst the lower section was of a rich black with vertical white bands. A somewhat similar decoration, but rather more sombre, was ASCOT which had a band of mauve roses on a black and white chequer band completed by a black ground body.

Another significant departure from established decorations was the **Lustrine** range, again launched in 1917. This was a more luxurious style incorporating gold prints and handpainting with patterns drawn from different subjects, as they were based on mythical and natural themes.

The general mood of change, exemplified by these decorations, was also reflected in the shape and type of articles produced. The large jardinieres and pedestals, so typical of Victorian and Edwardian households, had waned in popularity and consequently were phased out. Vases and flowerpots, albeit in simpler forms, retained their appeal whilst floating flower bowls were particularly in vogue. Wide and shallow with a slightly in-turning rim, this shape was especially suited for the new styles of decoration.

Decorating methods and the pattern motifs used continued to progress during the 1920's. Further lustre patterns were introduced whilst the black background was utilised with a greater variety of designs, for example DAISY in 1922 and MAVIS in 1926. Also indicative of these changes was the noticeable shift away from lithographic prints towards print and enamelled decorations for tablewares, a typical example of which was the CHELSEA BIRD design. This transition found favour with the Pottery Gazette whose correspondent stated feelingly that :

> *.... the colours show up with a brightness which comes as a real relief from some of the flatish conglomerations consisting of half a dozen colours or more crowded into a border of half an inch or less which have operated to the detriment of the lithographic process as a medium for pottery decoration.*

The late 1920's heralded the first buds of the major changes of style that were to blossom fully during the 1930's. The ERA shape, introduced in 1928, was modelled en-suite providing a comprehensive range of tablewares. Somewhat angular in shape, the

Examples of toilet and ornamental wares with black vellum grounds showing the Cedric pattern (top) and the Ascot pattern (bottom), 1920.

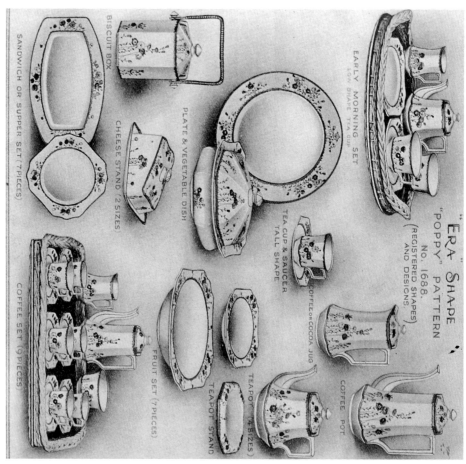

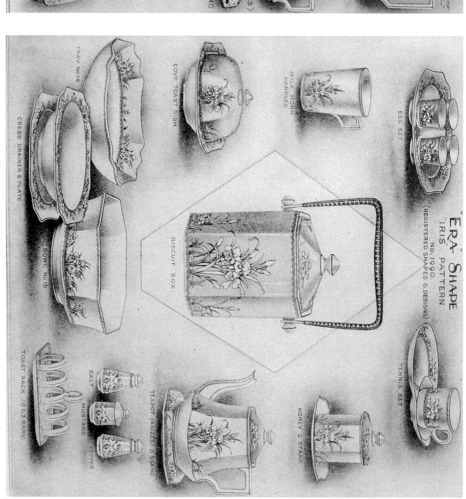

Two selections from the Era shape en-suite ranges for the Iris and Poppy patterns, 1928-1930.

Crown Devon gives that keynote of individuality which makes an instant
appeal to lovers of pottery who desire dignity of design at moderate cost.

Crown Devon

S. FIELDING & CO., LTD., DEVON POTTERY, STOKE-ON-TRENT

AGENTS :

NEW ZEALAND: John
Raine, Ltd., Thornton
Buildings, 66 Manners
St., Wellington.

CANADA : Parsons
Steiner, 60/2 Front St.
West, Toronto, 2

SOUTH AFRICA: L.A.
Solomon, 8 Progress
Lane, off Strand St., P.O.
Box 267, Capetown.

LONDON: A. J.
Holdcroft, 75 Gamage
Buildings, Holborn, E.C.

AUSTRALIA : W. E.
Bird, Ltd., 737G G.P.O.,
Sydney, New South
Wales.

1930's advertising leaflet.

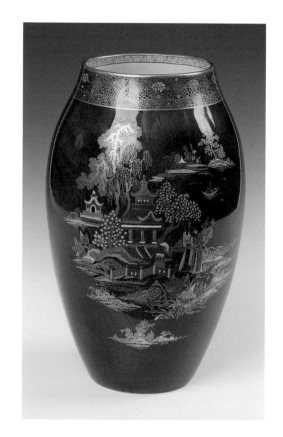

A richly enamelled orientally inspired pattern, overprinted and finished in gold on a powder blue background.

Orange lustre enamelled wall plaque, overprinted and finished in gold, 1930's.

A selection of powder blue ornamental wares including the Fantasia pattern (vase, top right) and a Vogue shape powder bowl (centre).

Examples of the best coffee sets finished with mother-of-pearl lustre.

Coffee and ornamental wares with the Orient pattern.

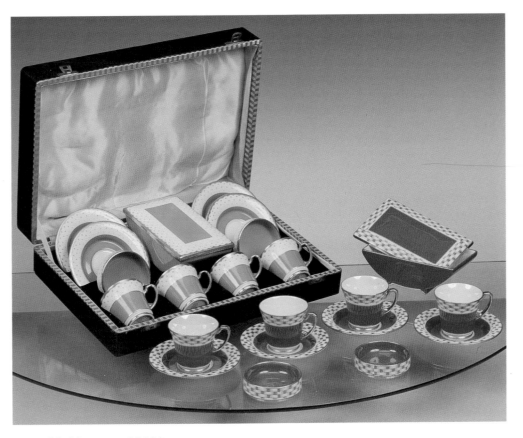

Boxed bridge sets, 1930's.

Examples of best coffee sets, finished in gold.

A range of matt glazed wares from the late 1930's and the 1940's including examples of the Regency shape (bowl, centre; vase, centre right and vase, top right).

Original promotional illustration for the Glenwood pattern with bright gold finish.

Coaching Days decoration as shown in a company brochure.

decorations were primarily based on brightly coloured floral patterns, such as POPPY and IRIS and these were applied using the print and enamel method.

Design Explosion (1930 - 1939)

The company's product portfolio was revolutionised from 1930. Two men, in particular, were responsible for the initiation of the major design campaigns which resulted in such a diversity of shapes, styles and decorations. They were Enoch Boulton, the Design and Decorating Manager and George Barker, the Sales Director both of whom joined the firm from Wiltshaw and Robinson in 1930. Their influence was felt in all areas from the high quality ornamental ranges to the innovative **Musical Novelties**.

Patterns were available to suit every taste and price range encompassing the spectrum of simple handcraft to elaborate enamelled and gilt decorations. Many different decorating techniques were employed to achieve this variety including handpainting, print and enamelling, tubelining, gilding and lustring.

The new patterns were complemented by new shape ranges. In ornamental wares, models featured both plain and ribbed bodies using angular forms, asymmetrical moulded ornamentations and embossed relief work to achieve their different effects. The product ranges encompassed vases, bowls, trays, table-centres, candlesticks, wall pockets, ginger jars and plaques.

For tablewares, the new conical shapes of MODANE and VOGUE epitomised the modern styling of the early 1930's and were used extensively. In addition, the **Embossed Tableware** ranges introduced in the late 1920's were progressively extended whilst many **Novelty Tableware** articles were also launched.

Matt glazes and grounds were used with a wide spectrum of designs, many of which were entirely handpainted. Described in advertisements as *'modern handcraft'*, these wares were said to *'enhance the beauty of the artistic home'*.

Flatbrush work with vivid colours was used to create the bold floral, geometric and banded patterns which reflected the most modern in popular taste. It is impossible to attribute the original inspiration for such trends but the Crown Devon designs certainly deserve recognition alongside the similar decorations produced by designers such as Clarice Cliff and Susie Cooper. It is also perhaps no co-incidence that A.E. Gray's factory was situated in close proximity to the Devon Pottery when their respective stylised floral patterns are compared. Recognising the popularity of such wares, the Pottery Gazette commented in October 1930 :

> *Gay though such decorations be, they represent what is being called for in many quarters just now, and they are assured of a ready sale.*

Other handcraft patterns drew their inspiration from more traditional sources, giving these an updated representation, as demonstrated in the DELPH series, which was based on the style of the Dutch potters. Another simple yet extremely effective design was CHECKS. Launched at the British Industries Fair in 1931, this was a deep border pattern for tableware which consisted of a series of pencilled lines in either yellow, pink, green or blue. The availability of matching table linen was reported to have found favour with Queen Mary who ordered tea and breakfast services in blue. The range was to retain its popularity for many years and was produced throughout the 1940's. Interestingly, visitors to Stanley Matthews' Blackpool hotel, after the war, would have had the pleasure of using yellow checks tableware.

A tubelined outline was utilised on patterns such as CHERRY TREE to enhance the handpainting and matt glaze. Described by the Pottery Gazette as 'a masterpiece of decoration', it featured a cherry tree in blue with fruit coloured in bright red against a brown background. Other tubelined decorations included an abstract pattern in blues and brown called CRETIAN and a floral design of red and green on a mottled brown ground known as GLENTONE. This latter pattern was featured strongly at the British Industries Fair in 1934 where it was shown on a large range of ornamental wares including pitcher shaped jugs, handled vases, plaques, lamps and bowls together with useful table articles such as dessert dishes and handled fruit baskets.

The significance of the matt glazed wares is indicated by the number of named ranges introduced, in particular MATTAJADE, MATTATONE and MATTITA, the name often being incorporated into the backstamp.

Mattajade was launched at the British Industries Fair in 1932 where it attracted considerable attention, not least from Queen Mary who purchased several items from the range. As its name suggests, it featured a matt ground of jade green formed into a circular pattern over which was applied entirely hand enamelled decorations often enhanced by a gold overprint. Examples of patterns in this range include CHINESE DRAGON, FLORAL ROCKERY and FAIRY CASTLES.

It is difficult to ascertain the distinguishing feature of the Mattita range as it encompasses a range of styles. However, known decorations include a bright cottage pattern on a yellow ground and DAFFODIL, also on a yellow background.

Mattatone, featuring running glaze effects, was introduced in 1934 when it was offered in four colours - brown, green, stone and a blend of blue and green. It was updated in 1936 by a series of multicoloured designs which embraced brown and blue, brown and green, and lemon and fawn.

Other matt-glazed ranges included PRUNELLA and AMAZINE. Prunella was executed in a variety of pastel shades in which a copper green predominated. The Pottery and Glass Record reported in 1932 that it was :

> .... of typically modern design that has never been done in this country before though the Germans have been doing it for years. Quite in the foreign style of decoration, Prinella (sic)ware is fired in a mouffle, giving an attractive matt glaze.

Amazine had a ground of soft blue, reminiscent of turquoise, to which richly enamelled patterns were applied. Typical of these was one depicting tropical flowers and trees with an exotic bird, overprinted in gold, over which the Pottery Gazette enthused :

It is an imposing pattern to be sure, and one that will be bound to meet with a ready sale in many markets. For its particular purpose, the producers themselves consider it to be one of the finest things they have ever brought out.

Many of the enamelled patterns were produced with a variety of backgrounds, powder blue and ruby lustre being particularly popular. For example, the Fairy Castles design was available on a choice of powder blue, Mattajade, ruby lustre, orange lustre or red lacquer grounds.

Another lavishly enamelled decoration was ORIENT, a striking abstract design with Modernist overtones in black, gold, green and red. In common with many of the more expensive patterns, this was applied to ornamental and coffee wares. Indeed, high quality coffee sets became a particular speciality with many of the decorations incorporating burnished gold or mother-of-pearl interiors and finishes. They were noted for the thinness of the body used leading Fielding's to claim that they were almost indistinguishable from china. The obvious suitability of such articles as gifts was fully exploited and a special feature was made of presentation boxed sets. Available in several compositions, the Smokers or Bridge Party sets proved particularly popular. These comprised four coffee cups and saucers, two ashtrays and a cigarette box arranged in a satin lined box.

In the medium price range, the print and enamel method provided a tremendous flexibility of design. A typical pattern of this type for tablewares was MORNING GLORIOUS which was printed in soft grey and enamelled up in bright colours. The design depicted the stepping stones of a garden with a colourful herbaceous border in the background. Other popular patterns were MEADOWSWEET which featured dainty sprays of spring flowers and DU BARRY which had a scattering of flowers with a suggestion of green grass.

A further variation in matt glazed wares was the use of embossed patterns. Since the pattern was an integral part of the shape, each of these ranges required their own exclusive moulds. However, this did not limit the choice available, as demonstrated by the MAYFIELD series, launched at the British Industries Fair in 1936, on twenty-five new shapes of vases, bowls and ornaments.

New tableware shape ranges were periodically introduced in the later 1930's, including BEVERLEY, BRAMLEY and RANLEIGH, all of which reflected the trend in design towards a rounder, softer profile. Beverley had a gently panelled and scalloped shape which remained popular for many years and it was used for a variety of different types of decoration.

Utility To Contemporary (1940 - 1959)

The 1940's was inevitably dominated by World War II and its aftermath. Government restrictions resulted in the Age of Utility with the home market being restricted to a limited number of shapes and only white and ivory ware. Export rejects provided the small amount of decorated articles that were available but these also were provided to retailers on a quota basis.

It is, therefore, not surprising that design style was primarily influenced by the requirements of the export markets. Simpler and softer patterns were in demand with the excesses of colour of the preceding years largely rejected in the sombre prevailing climate. The appeal of traditionally based decorations was a recognised factor in overseas trade and came to the fore during this period. However, it should be remembered that the most popular pre-war ranges continued to be produced throughout the 1940's, particularly from 1946 when the factory needed to gear up production quickly.

The REGENCY ornamental range, introduced in 1939, typified the progression of matt glazed wares. It had more elaborately moulded shapes based upon a period type of form although modified to suit modern furnishing schemes. The decorations were principally in pastel shades with gold finishes and the patterns comprised restrained, naturalistic motifs such as a stem of fern or corn. Interestingly, within two years, the range was given a totally different treatment with the application of chintz based patterns. Amongst the limited number of new designs of this period was a series of seven tray designs, three of which featured variations of the established subjects of dogs, pheasants and hunting and which were painted by Walter Lamonby.

The tableware ranges mirrored the design changes occurring in the ornamental lines. Two tree landscape patterns, GLENWOOD and SPRINGWOOD, were introduced in 1939 and could be viewed as examples of the transition in style. They both became very popular, selling successfully for many years. Another treatment also caught the buyers attention. This employed self-coloured pastel glazes in either single solid colours or dual tones, i.e. one self colour on the outside with a toning shade on the inside, finished with a gold edge and handle.

LYNTON was a new shape, introduced in 1944. It was initially available with two new patterns, both of which drew their inspiration from traditional motifs. The CABLE design was offered in a choice of maroon or grey, lined in gold on an ivory ground. The other pattern, unnamed, had a formal decorative unit alternating with a delicately treated floral spray, prompting the Pottery Gazette to remark that it :

Creates a definite impression of refinement and grace.

All restrictions on decorated wares were finally lifted in August 1952 and, although there was an increase in consumer spending as people restocked, the difference was not as great as the manufacturers had hoped and expected.

Attitudes to tablewares were changing with the public requiring greater flexibility. The custom of buying large elaborate sets was disappearing to be replaced by the

Embossed Stag design, 1950.

Sailor's Farewell decoration, 1950.

practice of starting with basic articles and adding the additional pieces to suit individual needs. This was particularly true of young couples setting up home with limited means. Living and eating habits generally were in a state of flux with a growing demand for 'modern' American style informal dinnerware.

Few factories had foreseen these trends although Reginald, with his extensive overseas travelling, was in a better position than most to appreciate the transcontinental influences. However, the introduction of new lines was significantly delayed because of the devastation reeked by the fire in 1951.

The new impetus to design was evident in many fields and developed into the Contemporary Style for which the 1950's is remembered. Shapes were fluid and often asymmetrical with few straight lines, reflecting a reaction to the severity of pre-war modernism. Patterns and colours were directed to meeting the wider interior design requirements and often incorporated a mix and match approach.

This design trend gathered momentum as the decade progressed. However, the early 1950's were dominated by the production of, and additions to, popular pre-war ranges. A typical example was the highly enamelled decorations applied to ruby lustre grounds. Those patterns depicting Chinese scenes were prominent although designs such as Fairy Castles and the Galleon also retained their popularity. New designs were also introduced to the series including HERALD and KINGFISHER.

Other designs were adapted to a different medium, for example the Champion Dogs series which had originally been modelled as a set of wall ornaments. In the mid-1950's, these formed the basis for a range of six service plate patterns which were printed in grey or brown and finished with a pearl glaze.

The inspiration for new designs was also drawn from historical sources as demonstrated by THE SAILORS FAREWELL pattern introduced in 1950. This was a reproduction of an old English print depicting the departure and return of a seafaring man. The decoration was underglaze printed and handpainted being finished in pink lustre bands and scrolls. The range was subsequently extended to incorporate different colourings and a variant was used for musical novelties. The pattern was available on bowls, cigarette boxes, jugs and trays.

The influence of the Contemporary style was shown in the introduction of the KAREN shape in 1955, named incidentally after Reg's daughter. New patterns were conceived to complement the shape which sometimes needed to overcome hesitancy on the part of the sales staff concerning their potential success. Perhaps the best known of these is STOCKHOLM, designed by Bill Kemp, which featured a red stag against a matt glaze background. This was based on the mural which had adorned the wall of the factory showroom prior to the fire. The green variant of the pattern was called GREENLAND. Other designs of this period include REYNARD which depicted a red fox in a snow scene, and STORM, a black abstract pattern on white. The Stockholm range was enormously successful leading to the inevitable imitation by other manufacturers, one of whom was Meakin whose variation was a black stag on a white background.

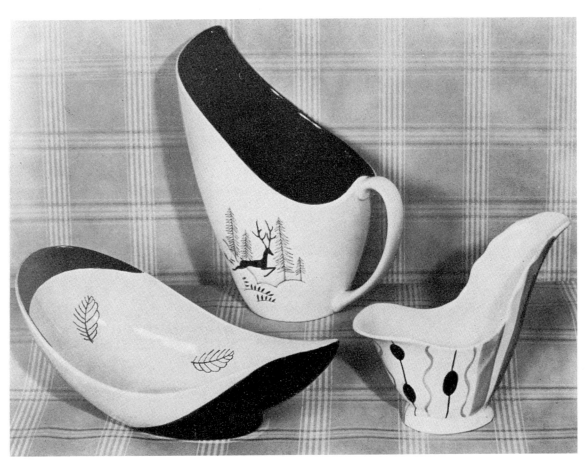

Contemporary designs, 1956.

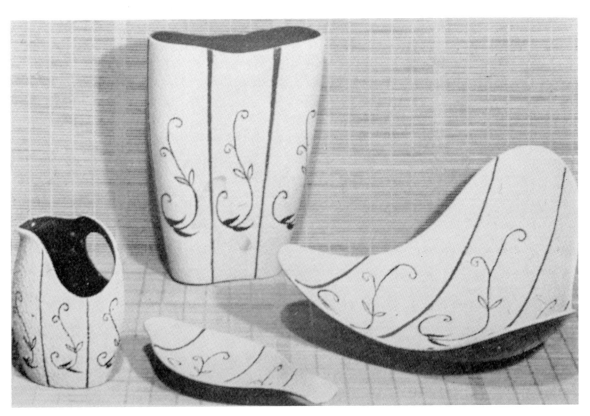

Hand painted design of black motif and red lines with red outsides to the dishes
and red inside the vases, on the matt white snowflake glaze.

In ornamental wares, the diversity of style was represented by designs such as PEGASUS, FI-FI, FLYING SWANS, SAILS and ANTIGUA. Pegasus was a finely drawn wild horses scene available in a range of decorative effects from white on black or selenium red, to ruby lustre grounds. It was to become a popular pattern, remaining in production for over twenty years. Antigua typifies the effect on design of changing lifestyles, in this case the increasing availability of foreign holidays to a wider population. The series comprised six stylised scenes depicting the beach, a pavement cafe, a donkey ride, sailing boats, a guitar player and dancer, and a fruit barrow. Printed in black on a mottled mushroom ground, the patterns were hand-enamelled in vibrant colours whilst the inside of the hollowares were aerographed in bright red.

The dangers of lead glazes had been known as early as the eighteenth century and had generated much debate prior to the final ban on their use in 1950. However, there was a growing realisation of other dangers, during the 1950's. In particular, that certain colours used in on-glaze decoration could react with acid food and release harmful elements. This resulted in an increasing use of under-glaze treatments and considerable research into alternative glaze compositions.

The matt white snowflake glaze was an immediate success when it was introduced at the Blackpool Fair in 1958, with the Pottery Gazette reporting that :

> An entirely new series of finishes was noted by some buyers to be the best that had been seen for many years.

This glaze was combined with a number of patterns, many of which were simple abstract designs, and applied to a range of the typically asymmetric shaped ornamental wares.

Ruby lustres; the vase and bowl (centre) are from the 1930's, the remaining items are post-war and include the Herald pattern (wall plaque, top) and the Kingfisher pattern (oval dish, bottom left).

A selection of Stockholm and Greenland tablewares with Stockholm vase (top left).

Wares produced between 1950 and 1982 including hand painted, embossed and transfer printed patterns combined with matt, high glaze and lustre finishes.

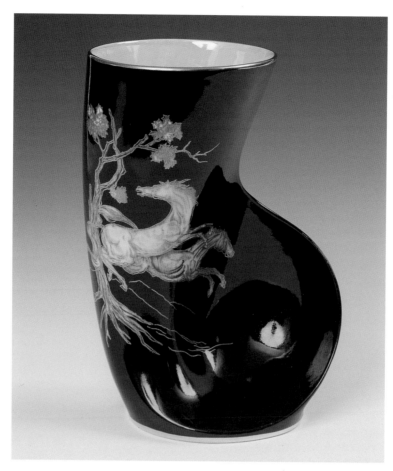

Pegasus pattern shown on an asymmetrical vase of the 1950's.

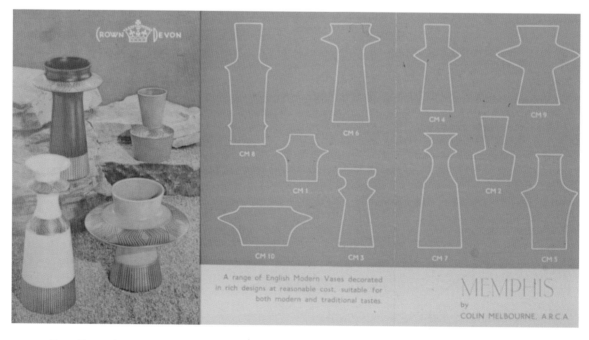

Retailer's leaflet for the Memphis range designed by Colin Melbourne, illustrating the ten shapes available.

Coffee sets of the 1960's; the Coronel shape designed by Colin Melbourne (left) and the Allegro shape with Pop Art pattern (right).

The Lowestoft range, introduced in 1968.

Transfer printed decorations including Cries of London (ginger jar, top left) and Christmas (centre right).

Advertising leaflet for a kitchenware range of the 1970's.

Retailer's leaflet for Charlotte, a popular and extensive range of the 1970's.

Pop Art And Nostalgia (1960 - 1982)

During the 1960's, the younger generation developed as a powerful consumer group with significant purchasing power. More than ever before, ceramics became fashion-orientated wares with a relatively short lifetime. These factors led to a plethora of styles reflecting the expanding scope of public taste, ranging from the popular imagery of graphic art to a growing nostalgia for Victorian design.

Matt or eggshell glazes retained their popularity into the early 1960's although they were increasingly combined with less strident colourings. Typical of this trend are patterns such as IVORY QUEEN which had a motif of ivory and pink roses with sage green leaves, and AUTUMN GLORY which reproduced a pencil sketch of the countryside in autumn colourings. These decorations continued to incorporate an element of handpainting to enhance the transfer print. All designs were available in a full range of dinner, tea and coffee services with other table accessories to match.

The Karen shape was remodelled in early 1965, the major modifications being made to the shape of the tea and coffee pots, to bring it up-to-date. However, the next major innovation in design was as a result of collaboration with Colin Melbourne.

The CORONEL shape tableware and MEMPHIS ornamental ranges were launched at a special show held at the Mount Royal Hotel, London in December 1963. The Coronel shape exhibited the most modern characteristics, the outline of the coffee pot, jug and vegetable dishes appearing low and having a recessed foot whilst the cups were tall. Nine patterns were available, eight of which were silk-screen decorations and one, a lithographic transfer. The CANBERRA pattern, in either green or brown, was made up of broken parallel lines interspersed with the freehand trails of a wandering star. MOONSTONE had a snowflake design on blue whilst on brown, it took the name of STARDUST. GOLDEN NILE featured a thick bronze-gold band overlaid with black lines of irregular length whilst three interlocking leaves comprised the ARDEN pattern. The brown or green all-over glaze of EVERGLADES was embellished with bands of black and white barley heads. The shape was also used for a fine white silk-screened fruit design applied to black exteriors. Further patterns were subsequently added to the range including VINE LEAF, which incorporated a black vine leaf motif with a copper-bronze band, and SGRAFFITO, an incised decoration in blue, green or brown.

The Memphis range of ten articles had a black and gold decoration available with white, black or blue and tan grounds. This did not prove to be a successful range and the shapes were subsequently re-issued decorated with plain yellow, blue, green and pink lustre finishes.

The decorations of another consultant, Chinese designer Ng Eng Teng, were featured the following year as part of a display at the Mostyn Hotel, London. The ZODIAC pattern incorporated the symbols for good and evil (Ying and Yang) and was produced on the Coronel shape in shades of blues and browns. The same designer was responsible for SPRING, a border of oriental style flowers. The show also provided the opportunity to launch additions to established ranges as well as the new designs. Maroon and blackberry coloured glazes were added to the Sgraffito series

Advertisement for the Ivory Queen design tableware, 1961.

Advertisement for the Vine Leaf decoration available on the Coronel shape range of tableware designed by Colin Melbourne, 1964/65.

Advertisements from the Pottery Gazette for the Florentine and Victoriana ranges.

and the white fruit motif on a black matt background with coloured interiors was extended to include teaware. The IONIC shape ornamental ware was also introduced in 1964. It was available with a variety of different patterns ranging from a print and enamelled fruit design embellished with bronze lustre bands to the striking OP ART decoration in black on a white background.

The two new ranges introduced at the Blackpool Fair in 1966 illustrate the company's response to the growing diversity of customer demand. The ALLEGRO shape with its tall cup and elongated coffee pot represented the trend towards cylindrical forms. Decorated with bold patterns such as LOTUS, this was the epitome of modern styling. In contrast, VICTORIANA appealed to those of a nostalgic leaning, drawing upon ornate mouldings and delicate prints embellished with gold to recreate a past age.

The popularity of historical sources was again evident two years later with the appearance of the LOWESTOFT series. This was an interpretation of the oriental style of decoration associated with the eighteenth century Suffolk pottery. It combined good domestic shapes with hand engraved and hand painted patterns. A total of six designs were available including ALDRED BLUE and ALLAN.

The product ranges of the mid to late 1960's also reflected the increasing influence of Douglas Bailey. His desire to shift the balance of manufacture towards mass production methods resulted in more collaborations with **commercial customers** and the re-introduction of cheaper cellulose wares through the subsidiary company, Baifield Productions Ltd. In an attempt to capture a larger share of the tableware market, the company departed from their traditional philosophies of quality and design, to produce a series of cheap eighteen piece teasets decorated with lithographic prints. However, these were not successful and were quickly discontinued.

In contrast to his attempts to introduce bulk product lines, Douglas Bailey also instigated a small unit to produce posy bowls of flowers. This was located in the saggar making shop which was no longer needed after the replacement of the bottle kilns. The posy bowls were handpainted by a team of 8 - 10 paintresses under the supervision of Mrs McGraw.

The FORM 500 range was launched at the Blackpool Fair in 1969. The range included tea and coffee ware and other table accessories as well as catering for the increasing popularity of oven-to-tableware items. New patterns were designed especially for the shape, many of which featured dark coloured glazes. These included JUPITER in a soft blue; DRUID, a black motif on a matt olive background; SUNBURST, a brown and yellow lithograph, and TAPESTRY which was a freehand design applied under a honey yellow glaze.

In a similar vein, the OMEGA shape appeared in 1972. Designed by John Cuffley, the resident designer, this was also of a 'chunky' appearance and reflected the popularity of the earthy stoneware derivatives at this time.

However, by the end of the 1970's, the mood was changing and styles were mellowing towards a rounder form with delicate pastel surface decorations. Fielding's continued to adapt the fashions of the past to meet the requirements of the present.

Jupiter pattern, Form 500 tableware.

Form 500 coffee pot, 1969/70.

Omega tableware designed by John Cuffley, 1972.

Ionic shape vase and Sgraffito tableware, 1964

Indeed, this aspect was often promoted in their advertising literature as seen in the leaflet for PRELUDE which stated :

Delicate pastel shaded and toning Victorian scroll combine with a lettered motif to produce an unusual design which captures the nostalgia of a bygone era, in this range of ornamental, gift and bathroom ware.

One particularly delightful innovation was the SEA SPRITE range of flower holders of the late 1970's. As the name suggests, some of these were modelled in the form of sea sprites, others as shells. They were finished in a white opaque glaze shaded inside with a delicate green. An alternative of white and gold was also available.

Another attractive range was launched at the International Spring Fair in 1980. MILLE FLEURS was an elegant embossed pattern of flowerheads in white, pink or grey. It was also available with a lustre finish and grey glaze giving a mother of pearl appearance.

It can be seen that the company continued to produce a significant range of articles throughout this period. Ornamental wares included ginger jars, planters and cache pots in addition to vases, trays and bowls. Tablewares had been progressively extended to cater for the diversity and individualism required by the buying public whilst new lines in bathroom, kitchen and gift wares provided scope for additional sales. Sadly, all of these activities were insufficient to stave off the effects of a deepening recession which finally forced the company's closure.

Majolica

Majolica, not to be confused with Italian maiolica, was one of the most popular styles of ceramic decoration in late Victorian households. Introduced by Minton at the Great Exhibition of 1851 in London, majolica wares have an earthenware body painted with, or dipped into, lead glazes. Further embellishment was sometimes added with gilding or handpainted enamels. The majority of majolica was relief-moulded although not all relief-moulded earthenwares decorated with lead glazes are majolica.

Initially, building on the product lines of F. Hackney & Co., a wide and varied range of articles was produced including umbrella stands, garden seats, lamps, dressing table sets, wall brackets and tablewares. Indeed, tablewares were produced in abundance and encompassed dinner and tea services, butter dishes, platters, mugs, moustache cups, pitchers, oyster plates, beer sets, dessert and ice sets, footed goblets and punch bowls.

A significant number of shapes and patterns were available from the old cloudy styles to new imitations of Beryl, Amethyst and other semi-precious stones. New designs and colourings were constantly added and of particular note were the Argenta (silver) wares, introduced in 1879. There has been some debate as to which factory should have the credit for the invention of Argenta colouring. Although Wedgwood introduced these wares in 1878 whilst Fielding's (as F. Hackney & Co) did not advertise them until a year later, this does not necessarily invalidate the Fielding claim. One answer to the discrepancy is that, as a type of colouring, Argenta was pioneered at the Fielding colour mill and supplied to Wedgwood as a customer.

Fielding's registered ten designs between 1881 and 1884, mostly for moulded jug forms. However, registration was not always a guarantee against imitation. During 1882, the firm brought an unsuccessful action against Hawley & Co for infringing their FAN design. Although morally the victors, they were unable to secure a verdict due to a technical oversight.

The Fan pattern was one of a number of popular designs, others being PANSY, FUSCHIA, RIBBON AND LEAF, SHELL AND NET, BRAMBLE, and DAISY. Argenta white was the most frequent background although alternatives included pale and cobalt blue, yellow, and grey. The use of textured backgrounds also added a welcome variety to their products.

The Shell and Net pattern, applied to a tea service, featured a raised net-like background and a multi-coloured variety of snail, conch and scallop shells entangled with brown-black seaweed, all caught in the net. Blue waves swirl at the base of each piece whilst the handles and spout simulate red coral and a small snail shell forms the finial.

The BOW AND FLORAL pattern had a rough, papillated background with borders of red, yellow, blue and white daisies or blue and pink morning glories around the base. White, pink, blue or yellow ribbons near the top of the article are tied in a bow. The Ribbon and Leaf design depicted leaves, strawberry blossoms, and a superimposed ribbon and bow on a well-modelled basket weave background.

An Oriental influence is seen in the various fan patterns which are set against both stippled and smooth backgrounds. Fans in multi-coloured designs are pleated or paddle-shaped, decorated with insects and butterflies and placed at random amongst prunus blossoms and stylised chrysanthemums.

A distinctive feature of the majolica produced at Fielding's was the effective way they introduced, on their best pieces, hand-modelled flowers and foliage with naturalistic colouring. A contemporary commentator, Jewitt, in his work 'The Ceramic Art of Great Britain' enthused :

> .... thrown in graceful negligence around the bodies of the vases, they become such perfect reproductions that it was difficult to divest the mind of the idea that the roses were not fresh gathered from the tree and temporarily twined around the vase for its adornment.

In contrast to these elegant and delicate patterns and in an interesting reflection of another aspect of the prevailing popular taste, the Pottery Gazette reported that :

> A large piece intended for an umbrella stand, with a dead hare and duck, in relief, hanging by the legs from the trunk of a tree which forms the receptacle for the umbrella, is a fine piece.

The firm regularly received favourable reports in the trade press for the quality and form of their products. A typical example is the following extract from the Crockery and Glass Journal of April 1882 :

> We were favoured with a view of several novelties, including a pair of umbrella stands formed by the trunk of a tree, against which is the figure of a skating girl just starting off on the ice. The 'Goat' umbrella stand gives promise of extraordinary merit. The general finish of their goods is excellent, and the colour is remarkably good.

In addition to supplying the home market, a considerable level of trade was developed with America where this style of decoration was, if anything, even more popular. However, majolica did not feature in the firm's advertisements from 1890 and was phased out of production during the 1890's.

The Royals

In order to compete successfully with the cheap foreign goods flooding onto the market, a policy of progressively introducing a higher class of product at low prices was put into place. This resulted in a series of decorative 'Art Ware' ranges which may collectively be termed 'The Royals'.

The first of these, launched in January 1890, was to become synonymous with the firm to such an extent that, ultimately, it brought about a change in the factory name. Initially introduced to the market as CROWN DEVON, within six months the name had been amended to ROYAL DEVON by which it was to be known for many years. The range caught the attention of the trade and buying public alike both in the home market and overseas, selling particularly well in America. In a period when new decorations were constantly demanded, it held its popularity and inevitably led to other manufacturers attempting to copy it. This unusual combination of factors was encapsulated in a report in the Pottery Gazette of March 1908 :

> *One of the most popular lines S. Fielding & Co produce is their 'Royal Devon Ware'. This, so far from becoming old, is I understand, selling better than ever. It has a very neat ornamentation, a pleasing combination of blue flowers and gold on cream ground. It is the quiet tone that is so pleasing in this choice decoration. Toilet ware, vases, flower pots, miscellaneous tableware, and fancy goods are all supplied in this ware. The style of 'Royal Devon Ware' has been copied. Of course, the company would rather they were not imitated but Mr Fielding himself does not seem much perturbed at the competition. He philosophically says, 'The imitations that are as good as ours in finish are dearer, and those that are the same price as ours are inferior in quality'.*

Encouraged by its success, further ranges were subsequently introduced. In April 1891, ROYAL WINDSOR was offered with the bold claim that it had the appearance of Royal Worcester at the price of common foreign glass. In order to achieve a wide distribution as rapidly as possible, the wholesale firms were courted with offers of special inducements if they promoted the range.

In September the same year, CROWN CHELSEA made its appearance - this was also to undergo a name change to ROYAL CHELSEA. This decoration featured a shaded matt ground in different combinations of colours with floral sprays heavily traced in gold.

By the end of the year, yet another range was available, ROYAL WESTERIAN, which seems to have been particularly aimed at the American market. The pattern again featured a delicately coloured floral spray, traced in gold with the handles finished off in burnished gold.

Three further ranges were introduced at the end of 1894 - ROYAL SUSSEX, ROYAL CLARENCE and ROYAL ESSEX. These patterns were applied to a great variety of shapes including art vases, flower pots and biscuit jars. Indeed, a key feature of all the 'Royal' decorations was their application to a wide range of articles.

The ROYAL YORK and ROYAL KEW designs first appeared in 1898, the former being described as 'a polyanthus in a bright cloudy style of colouring which is very effective'. These were followed a year later by the new decorations of ROYAL TUDOR (applied to vellum grounds), ROYAL PERSIAN and ROYAL OXFORD.

It is interesting to note that there continued to be a certain fluidity in the naming of patterns. For example, Royal Persian had a name change to ORIENT whilst Royal Oxford had originally been produced as CARNATION. Variations of these patterns were entered into the pattern books up to 1903. Indeed, in some cases, completely different designs were launched under an existing name. One such instance was a new Royal York decoration featuring handpainted yellow roses which was brought out in 1903. However, the largest number of different designs were produced under the Royal Chelsea name and it would appear that this name, at least, referred to a style of decoration rather than to one particular pattern.

Three further Royals were to make their debut - ROYAL OSBORNE in late 1902, ROYAL DELFT in early 1903 and ROYAL GUELPH in September 1910. The latter two of these differ from the other Royals in that the patterns were executed underglaze in darker colours and were completed with a high glaze rather than the more usual matt finish. ROYAL GUELPH was a series of patterns, mainly featuring figure subjects, which appear to have been designed for pairs of wares. Guelph is taken from the name of the Dukes of Bavaria, a distinguished princely family now represented by the Ducal House of Brunswick and the British royal family. 1910 saw a change in the monarchy with the death of Edward VII and succession of George V and perhaps this prompted the use of such an unusual series name.

Finally, and somewhat of an anomaly, the Pottery and Glass Record of 1926, reporting on the Fielding stand at the British Industries Fair, refers to a Royal Kew vase of some 15 inches decorated with eagles and mountain scenery.

Pearline, Silverine and Gold

Pearline and Silverine were two of a series of ranges which aimed to imitate or reproduce the visual effect of natural materials.

A representation of silver had been available as early as 1879 in the Argenta ware, initially produced by Hackney, Kirkham & Co and continued by Fielding's after the take-over. In addition, the CRYSTALINE range, introduced in 1887, had a background of a dull textile appearance against which the decorations had the soft effect of water colours, being particularly noticeable in the landscape scenery designs.

However, it was with Pearline and Silverine that considerable success was achieved and a continuing trend for this style of decoration was established.

Pearline was introduced in 1900 with additions to its range being made periodically through to (at least) 1915. As its name suggests, the effect was of a pearl-like irridescence which was very appropriate to embossed shapes. It was applied to tableware en-suite including such items as teapots, biscuit jars and salad bowls. However, it was particularly effective on larger articles such as toilet sets. The Pottery Gazette of October 1900 remarked that :

> This Pearline has a good appearance when shown under, or adjacent to, a good light, either electric or incandescent. A few sets of this would brighten up a stock wonderfully.

In the Silverine range, Fielding's had an immensely popular product which sold strongly for over forty years. Introduced in 1910, this imitation of silver was first applied to teaware, in particular the Queen Anne shape. The silver effect was further enhanced by matt black handles which had the appearance of wood.

This style of decoration caught the attention of King George V and Queen Mary on their visit to the Potteries in 1913 with the King anxious to find out how it was produced. During the Queen's subsequent visit with her daughter, Princess Mary, to the associated exhibition at Harrods, the Pottery Gazette reported that :

> Princess Mary was delighted with the Silverine ware and was surprised to hear that it would not tarnish similarly to the silver of which it was a representation.

The range was progressively extended until virtually any article traditionally made in silver plate was available in Silverine. Items included tea and coffee sets, cruets, cake and egg stands, cheese and butter dishes, sardine boxes, salvers, rose bowls, sauce tureens, toastracks and candlesticks. The Pottery Gazette of November 1917 enthused :

> As displayed on the showroom shelves, this ware eminently justifies the high praise which it has won.

Two other variations were also available at the top of the Silverine range. The first was the standard ware but gold-lined whilst the second was scalloped pieces reproducing the effect of a hammered surface.

Exhibited regularly at trade fairs throughout its lifetime, the range was produced until the end of the 1950's.

In a similar vein, a new series was introduced in the early 1960's, called GOLD. The idea for this decoration is said to have resulted from a visit to Stoke market by a member of staff. There he saw a stall selling brass which, from a distance, gave the effect of gold. Ornamental wares and a limited range of tablewares, including a coffee set and a cruet, were available. The long-established Queen Anne shape teapot, formerly used for Silverine, was also utilised for Gold. The range was promoted as giftware, particularly suitable for anniversaries and weddings, with each article being individually wrapped and boxed. It was a popular line which was produced for many years, a measure of its success being shown by its imitation by Grimwade's.

A selection from the Gold range, 1963.

The Artists

Fielding's had concentrated on a policy of producing good quality wares, at reasonable prices, for the 'medium class' market. Having been very successful with this approach, attention was increasingly directed at more high class decorations which reached fruition towards the end of 1911.

Handpainting had been a feature of Devon products for many years, limited to a 'touching up' of lithographs on the lower value designs progressing to a full print and enamel technique on their more elaborate decorations.

Obviously, artists had been employed from the outset but unfortunately there is no detailed record of these early craftsmen. However, an obituary to Thomas Bott in the Pottery Gazette of February 1898, lamenting his death at the early age of 36, described him as a clever artist working at Fielding's having previously been employed at Royal Worcester. It is also known that Mr Wagstaffe was a senior artist at the works in 1903 since it was he who decorated the illuminated address presented to Abraham Fielding and his wife on the occasion of their silver wedding. Details obtained from the Staff Salaries Book indicate that he was still employed by the company in 1926.

The earliest association of artists to particular decorations is the Soleilian range, introduced in 1904, some pieces of which carry the signature of Lucas or Debray.

A team of artists seems to have been assembled, each having their own subject specialisations. Interestingly, it is only occasionally that a specific artist is designated to a particular design in the pattern books - the more usual notation being *'painted by men'*.

Apart from a WILD ROSE design in 1907/8, the first series of patterns was introduced during the years 1911 to 1914 with subsequent additions in the early 1920's. However, it is known that these wares continued to be produced in the intervening period because they were shown at exhibitions. One example is the British Industries Fair in 1917 from which the Pottery Gazette reported :

> *Ivory vellum almost monopolised the centre stand and included a row of large and shapely vases of exhibition class. Some of these were embellished with handpainted panels by expert artists depicting landscapes and animals, the shaggy Highland Cattle being a favourite subject. Similar paintings were also shown in frames for wall decoration.*

These decorations were produced by the print and enamel method, that is a printed transfer outline was applied to the ware as a guide for the extensive handpainting; the mounts, handles and edges being finished in gold. In addition to the large range of art vases and the decorative slabs for framing, toilet, table and dessert wares were also available.

Decorations were predominantly based on natural subjects such as flowers, birds and animals. Patterns during this period included roses, peacocks, game birds, storks, sheep, stags, highland cattle and dogs.

Many talented painters executed these patterns including Hancock, Coleman, Cox and Hinton. However, special mention must be made of Walter Lamonby who worked at Crown Devon from 1912 until his death in 1952 and who was, for the greater part of this time, in charge of the men painters. He had been an outstanding pupil at the Stoke School of Art, serving his apprenticeship with George Jones & Sons Ltd and had worked for John Aynsley & Sons prior to joining the Devon Pottery.

Artists were also associated with some of the Lustrine range, introduced in 1917. Two known examples are a fruit design on a blue background signed by G. Brough and a wall plaque depicting a Fielding family dog, Simon of Trentham, painted by Lamonby.

By the end of the 1920's, the vellum style of decoration had waned in popularity although a limited range continued to be produced. However, three designs based on the earlier style, depicting ducks, grouse and pheasants were introduced in the mid-1930's. These were painted by Lamonby and were produced on coffee bridge sets and bridge sets. Two further patterns followed, the first of which was a hunting scene of a rider and hounds whilst the second was a new adaptation of the Pheasants pattern. Each of these designs had their own backstamp, TALLY-HO and PHEASANTS respectively, and both were painted by Lamonby.

It must be remembered that the men painters worked on a variety of wares, not all of which carry a signature. For example, it was the men who undertook the painting of the musical novelty ranges from their introduction in the 1930's.

Another talented painter, Thomas Wilcox, joined Fielding's as an apprentice in 1934 at the age of 14 and worked there until 1962. He recalls that the artists worked in part of a warehouse and special efforts had to be made to reduce the dust levels around the wares. His painter colleagues at this time were William Stockley, Sidney Walker, George Shore, Joseph Clewes, Kenneth Quarmby, George Stretch, George Gibson, Arthur Wood, Jack Fenn and Stanley Dunn.

Tom Wilcox with one of three covered vases made for the Football Association of Wales to commemorate matches played on the continent during May 1953, for presentation to the French and Yugo-Slav Football Associations.

126

Lustrine

With the end of the First World War in prospect, a mood for change was growing and this was reflected in the demand from the buying public for new styles of decoration in all fields. One aspect of this demand was met by the Lustrine range of ornamental wares. This was conceived towards the end of 1917 and effectively launched at the British Industries Fair in February 1918.

The initial series of ten patterns depicted primarily mythical and natural subjects such as The Queen of the Fairies, Mermaids, Lizards, and Leopards. The range quickly caught the attention of the trade press which remarked upon the technical excellence that had been achieved, particularly in the colour tones. These favourable reactions are further highlighted by the following detailed report which appeared in the Pottery and Glass Record in May 1919 :

> It is called Mavis because this bird forms the leading figure of the decorative scheme, both externally and internally. There is an edging and inner broken scroll border of gold, with filling of Indian blue under the glaze, on which are the outlined figures of the Mavis bird and game cock, relieved with running floral sprays and stars, the bodies of petals and of the birds being grass green and nut brown. Internally, the most successful colour effects are executed, the body glaze being of a golden orange scintillating the whole scheme and lighting up the figures. Here the richest effect is on the game cock with its sea green plumes and deep orange and yellow neck, breaking away into variegated greens and nut browns at tail. In the centre is a geometric circular design on the lines of celtic work with sea green tintings at (the) scalloped border and centre radiations of variegated green and purple hues lit up by gold ray effects. There is an interlaced outer border in gold.

For the British Industries Fair in 1920, a WILLOW Lustrine design was offered in several different colours, principally saxe-blue, yellow, orange, green and purple, of which purple was the latest addition. A display of several large pieces, some decorated with Chinese inspired lustres, was also featured.

The RUSTINE variation to the range was introduced at the same exhibition the following year. This featured a russet-brown background with a black border and a Chinese Lantern theme in oriental colours. It was supplied en-suite from small fancies through to toiletware.

The British Empire Exhibition at Wembley in 1924 provided the impetus for both new designs and product shapes. Two patterns, in particular, generated considerable interest. SYLVAN had handpainted butterflies applied to a rich maroon ground relieved by a network of gilding. ROYAL GEORGE was a pictorial representation of the historic sailing ship and was applied to a blue ground.

The Pottery Gazette previewing the new ranges was enthusiastic :

Some of the new floating flower bowls which have been produced at the Devon Pottery for display at the British Empire Exhibition at Wembley are really sumptuous as regards colourings and lustrings, whilst the distribution and balance of the decorations leave nothing to be desired.

Several new patterns were launched in 1926. The first of these, BIRCH, was an artistic interpretation of the characteristics of the birch tree and was available with, or without, the addition of a butterfly. This pattern was produced as both a lustred and non-lustred decoration, although in both cases, it was applied using the print and enamel technique. Building on the success of Sylvan and Royal George, new treatments of similar subjects were introduced in the RUBY TROPICAL and RUBY VIKING designs.

The range of applied decorations was regularly updated to ensure a continued interest and consequent longevity. In total, over a hundred patterns and variations are recorded in the pattern books encompassing such diverse subjects as English Cattle, Fruit Wreaths, Chinese Pagodas, Dragons, and Birds. All Lustrine pattern numbers are prefixed by the letter 'L' and the series name is incorporated into the backstamp.

The series sold successfully throughout the 1920's and continued into the 1930's. The prominent position that it occupied in the company's displays at exhibitions during this period has been previously indicated.

Success at home was matched by significant acclaim overseas. A typical example being the award of a diploma and silver medal to the company for their display of Lustrine ware at the New Zealand and South Seas Exhibition held at Dunedin, New Zealand in 1926.

Embossed Tablewares

The use of embossed details as ornamentation was a well established design practice and often provided the identifying characteristics of particular shape ranges. However, it is those decorations in which the pattern was an integral part of the shape moulding that are considered here. A number of these embossed and handpainted ranges were periodically introduced, many of which incorporated a novelty element. They were offered in a comprehensive selection of useful table and/or salad wares.

Perhaps the best known of these are the SAVOY tomato and lobster series which, from their introduction in the late 1920's, retained their popularity for many years and still featured strongly on the company's stand at the Blackpool Fair in 1958. The basic form was a background of lettuce leaves, in a choice of green or primrose, with realistically modelled tomatoes or lobsters coloured in bright red. A tremendous variety of articles was produced including the usual bowls, trays and plates. However, in addition, there were several styles of cruets, a sectioned hors d'oeuvre dish, a cress dish and stand, and even a sauce bottle holder.

A number of new decorative treatments were applied to the range during the post-war years, creating new images for an established product and primarily aimed at extending their ornamental appeal. This is particularly demonstrated by one variation in which the tomatoes were painted in gold against green, primrose or the new plum coloured backgrounds, whilst the red tomatoes on a black background was an equally striking combination. Another innovation transformed the tomatoes into orange or red plums which were again available on a choice of green or primrose grounds.

Different background patterns such as a vine leaf or woven basketwork were offered as an alternative to the lettuce leaves, although these were available on a more limited range of articles. Similar designs of the 1930's included leaf dishes with a rabbit or squirrel perched on one edge and a pattern incorporating green vine leaves with bunches of purple and pink grapes set on a primrose coloured background.

As the name suggests, fruit formed the basis of the ORCHARD series which was introduced in 1929. Combined with floral and leaf motifs and with a woven wicker background, it was handpainted in natural tints on a warm ivory coloured body. Remaining in production until the 1950's, the wide range of tablewares was supplemented by matching ornamental articles in the later years bearing testament to the popularity of the design. Several colour variations were also introduced from 1949 including a straw glaze, pastel colourings and a black background whilst a pearl glaze was combined with green aerographing and undecorated fruit.

Three other embossed patterns of the 1930's were FLORENTINE, FLORA and BELLE FLEUR, all of which utilised a primrose glaze. Florentine and Flora were offered with a choice of colourings whilst the poppies, pansies and snapdragons of Belle Fleur were decorated naturalistically. A typically wide selection of wares was available in each of these designs encompassing such items as teapots, trays, fruit baskets and honies. Florentine was to prove the most enduring of these ranges being produced until the 1970's.

Advertisement from the Pottery Gazette of 1948 for the Garden range.

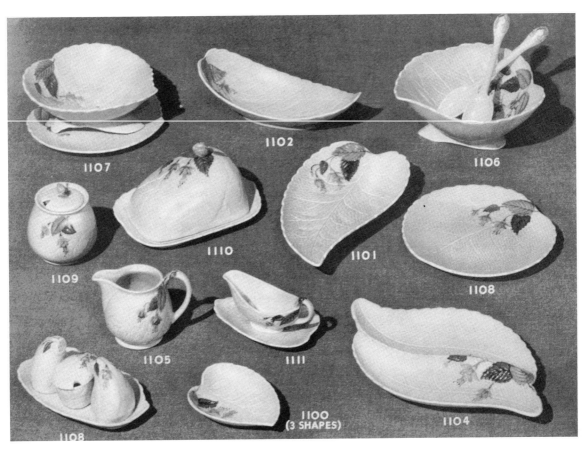

The Fuchsia range of embossed tablewares, 1958.

The Tropicana range of embossed tablewares, 1961.

131

It was particularly versatile as a plate border being easily combined with a variety of centre patterns to create a diversity of styles.

The GARDEN range was first shown at the British Industries Fair in 1939 and again proved to be very popular, providing good export orders from many countries throughout the 1940's and 1950's. The design comprised a background representing crazy paving overlaid with sprays of flowers. Initially available with a cream glaze, a number of variations were later introduced including the addition of a green edge or panel, primrose or green backgrounds, and a pale green background edged in gold. In each case, the colours of the flowers were selected to effectively compliment the background. The decoration was available on a large range of fancy articles such as cheese dishes, cruets, sugar dredgers, fruit sets, salad bowls, trays, toast racks and teasets, some of which could be purchased individually boxed. It was further extended to encompass purely ornamental wares for which a matt white glaze was used to particular effect.

A simpler design, ELEGANCE, made its appearance in 1953. This featured delicately tinted flowers on a primrose glaze with the finials and parts of the handles also being formed as flowerheads. Alternative colourways were soon available including green and peach backgrounds, but perhaps the most notable had the flowers painted in black and coral red contrasting with a straw coloured background. A further four variations were introduced in 1961 - a mother of pearl lustre finish, and grey, shaded pink and green background colours.

The mid-1950's also saw the introduction of FISH ware which remained in production until the factory closed. Each item was modelled in the form of fish and was available in several colours. The range comprised various dishes and plates together with a sauce boat and cruet. A lamp base was also added for a time but this was subsequently discontinued.

The FUCHSIA decoration was introduced in 1957, the flowers of which were handpainted in striking natural colours of pink and lavender accompanied by green leaves, disposed on either a mushroom or grey glaze background.

The Blackpool Fair in 1961 witnessed the launch of the TROPICANA range which was inspired by tropical flowers, emulating them in the brilliant reds, blues and greens. Originally produced with a beige matt glaze, the series was extended with several other finishes including pearl and straw glazes with mother of pearl lustre, a white matt glaze and an underglaze pink background.

Crown Devon continued to produce embossed tablewares until its closure, interestingly employing essentially the same decorating techniques as had been used over the previous fifty-plus years.

As an advertising leaflet for the FRUIT pattern of the late 1970's declared :

> *Tableware with a difference. It is available in green, yellow or plain white, is underglaze freehand painted and aerographed, processes which help to achieve the interesting relief on the many items available in the range.*

Novelty Table and Kitchen Wares

Although shaped tablewares, such as leaf and cucumber trays, had been produced from the turn of the century, it was not until the late 1920's and more especially the 1930's, that the extensive range of imaginative novelty items was first conceived. Similar articles had previously been the forte of continental manufacturers but Crown Devon were able to compete successfully by producing better quality articles at a lower price. These wares were to remain a significant part of the company's business until its closure. However, whatever the period, the essence of the designs was purely and simply FUN!

Table accessories, such as cruets and preserves, formed a part of the en-suite ranges, particularly the embossed wares, but many individual designs were also available. A popular theme of the Thirties was the use of buildings and their environments, typified in the VILLAGE cruet which had a representation of an old inn as the salt, a windmill as the mustard and a draw-well as the pepper. The Pottery Gazette commented :

> The cruet stand has an embossment giving a cobbled street effect to make the spirit of the old village complete.

In a similar vein, a cheese dish in the form of an olde worlde cottage with gables and a red roof was humourously entitled THE CHEDDAR CHEESE. The complementary biscuit box with a cane handle was called THE BAKER'S INN but, unfortunately, the name of the matching preserve pot is unknown.

The COTTAGE cruet was formed by the pepper in the left wing, the salt in the right wing and the mustard as the main building in the centre. A summerhouse mustard with a sundial pepper and a fir tree as the salt made up the GARDEN cruet whilst the FLORAL set featured a tulip mustard, pansy salt and marigold pepper.

In a somewhat different style, the COCKEREL and DUCKLING cruets each featured a figure of the respective bird with eggs forming the condiment containers. There was also a Duckling eggset comprising four eggcups with two eggs acting as pepper and salt. The CHICK eggset had a similar composition and, as on all of these, a figure of the bird served as the handle.

Amongst the many preserve pots were beehive honey jars and honeycomb honey boxes together with JAFFA orange marmalade pots. The Jaffa range was subsequently extended to include juice squeezers, a large jug and beakers (available individually or as a seven piece lemonade set) and a tea for two set. All were available in two colours, orange or lemon.

A range of novelty storage jars was first shown at the Blackpool Fair in 1957. These were primarily designed as cookie or biscuit jars although the advertisements promoted them as ideal gifts for both children and adults by suggesting other uses such as for cereals or bath salts. There were six models in the range, the Perky Pup and Scottie being adaptations of the popular animal figures introduced in the thirties. The range proved popular and was particularly well-received in the Canadian market.

133

Another novelty which was ideally suited to the giftware market was the jumbo cup and saucer, produced from the mid-1950's. These were typically decorated with amusing patterns such as adaptations of mythological scenes and cartoons. However, more elaborate decorations were also utilised, for example the gold lustre OLDE ENGLAND pattern, designed by Robin Gray. In contrast, others played blatantly on sentimentality in order to achieve sales as in the case of those inscribed with 'Mother' and 'Father'.

Suiteware had included a cup and integral plate, known as a tennis set, since the 1920's when it was designed to facilitate outdoor eating and drinking. Afternoon tea parties in the garden may have declined as a social activity by the 1950's but watching television was certainly on the increase. As a result, the article was re-instated as a TV set and given a new lease of life. The decorations used, such as two bright contrasting colours or black stripes on either white, yellow or blue backgrounds, epitomised the contemporary style.

The late 1950's also saw the emergence of a different type of salad ware which was also marketed as barbecue or casual table wares. The colourful applied decorations used the print and enamel method and were originally designed to have a white background and a high glaze finish. However, this was considered too stark for the home market and was subsequently modified to a mottled matt oyster glaze. A gay vegetable pattern, called PANACHE, was introduced in 1957 whilst, two years later, the OCEANIA design combined lobster, seahorse, starfish and crustacean motifs to good effect. However, it was humour that was to the fore in 1960 with the GAIETY GRILL series designed by E. Miles-Knowles. This depicted a barbecue scene with the personnel including sausages, cabbages and carrots. Several new patterns were introduced during the following years, in particular TAMPICO in 1963 which was executed in the Latin American style having wine carafes, glasses, tropical fruit, garlic and chicken amongst the images used.

New cruets in the shape of cacti and toadstools were introduced in 1961 alongside preserve pots embossed with squirrels and floral decorations or modelled as lobster pots. These were decorated underglaze and the advertisements proclaimed the qualities of their 'acid resisting colours' which reflected the increasing awareness of the inherent dangers of traditional decorating methods.

GHOST TOWN was the name of a set of storage jars available in the late 1970's. As the name suggests, the four jars represented buildings in a Western town namely, The First City Bank, Last Chance Hotel and Saloon, the General Store and the Sheriff's Office. Again, they were marketed as having a wide appeal as gifts for all ages.

The International Spring Fair in 1980 was used to launch additions to the CITY GENT and COWBOY ranges and to introduce the POLICEMAN series. These were all designed exclusively for Fielding's by J & G Morten as indicated on the backstamps which incorporate a copyright text. The Cowboy and City Gent were available as a variety of bathroom and tablewares, a feature of the Cowboy cream jug and teapot being their handles which were modelled as sixguns. The Policeman range of tableware comprised nine items - teapot, milk, sugar, teacup and saucer, bowl, small plate, tumbler and footed eggcup.

Series of novelty biscuit jars, 1957.

The same fair also saw the introduction of a kitchenware range decorated with a design by a seven year old, Catherine Simcock. This was the winning entry in a competition organised by the company in conjunction with local primary schools. Entitled HOLIDAYS, it depicted a lively scene of travellers with their luggage about to board a train at the station. Executed in bold, bright colours, the design was applied to storage jars, coffee and tea pots, cheese and butter dishes, jugs, mugs and rolling pins.

The following year, in the company's last appearance at the International Spring Fair, further new novelties by J & G Morten were on display. Amongst these was a FARMERS WIFE cheese dish and matching cruet which had a handpainted finish decorated to give the appearance of stoneware. Other items included a THREE-MEN-IN-A-BOAT cruet set together with cheese dishes modelled as both a SCHOOL BELL and a STRAW BOATER.

Tampico barbeque and salad ware, 1963.

Novelty cruets and preserve pots, 1961.

Advertising leaflet for tomato and lobster embossed salad wares in green and primrose glazes.

Orchard embossed tablewares.

INTRODUCE

"*Elegance*"

With its dignified shapes and charm of colouring this exquisite range of
table fancies wins instant appeal

Elegance embossed tablewares, 1953.

Retailer's leaflet for the Fish range.

Retailer's leaflet for the embossed Fruit range.

140

Advertising leaflet showing a selection of embossed and novelty tablewares.

Novelty tablewares including a Perky Pup biscuit jar (top left) and a Mother Christmas kitchen tidy (top right).

141

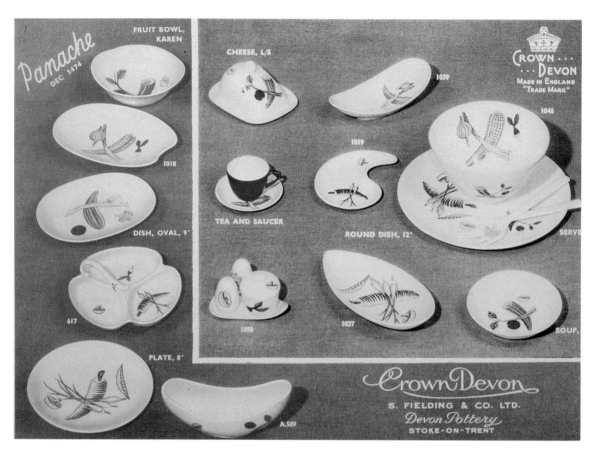

Retailer's leaflet for the Panache range.

Novelty salad wares including Gaiety Grill (left), Oceania (top right and centre) and Panache (bottom right).

142

Novelty giftware including the Farmer's Wife cheese dish and cruet (top left), School Bell cheese dish (top right) and Straw Boater cheese dish (bottom left).

Ghost Town storage jars.

Jumbo cup and saucer with the Olde England lustre pattern designed by Robin Gray.

Novelty teapots from the Cowboy, City Gent and Policeman ranges.

144

China

Fielding's was an earthenware manufacturer, as were F. Hackney & Co before them. Hence, the limited references to china wares which appear in the pattern books, trade reports and advertisements are somewhat of an enigma.

The earliest reference identified is an advertisement of 1879, placed by F. Hackney & Co, which included china in a general list of their products. No further mention is made until 1896 when the Pottery Gazette reported on the availability of *'some very pretty and neat patterns in china tea and breakfast sets'*. This is re-inforced the following year by an illustrated advertisement featuring china teasets.

The pattern book entries relating to commemorative wares for the coronation of Edward VII in 1902 include a china mug. This was decorated with a lithographic transfer of the King and Queen augmented by sprays of rose, thistle and shamrock.

The pattern books are also the source of an undated separate listing of fifteen patterns for application to china cups (see below). However, this would appear to be incomplete since two other patterns have been recorded, i.e. C47 - Jersey and C51 - Turin. It would be reasonable to conclude that, at least, some of the intervening numbers in the sequence were also utilised.

The last available reference dates from 1933. Five entries in the pattern books indicate china teaware, the last two of which have matching earthenware coffee sets and dinnerware.

In the absence of recorded facts, it can only be a matter of speculation whether china was ever manufactured at the Sutherland Street factory. However, given that the processes for china and earthenware are significantly different, it is more likely that the whiteware was always bought-in and decorated in-house, probably to match the firm's own earthenware patterns, as was the case from the 1930's onwards.

With the exception of the commemorative mug, it seems clear that pattern numbers for china wares had a letter 'C' prefix.

Toilet wares from an advertisement in the Pottery Gazette, 1917.

Toilet Wares

Toilet wares were produced from the inception of the pottery until the late 1920's. Comprised principally of ewers and basins, optional extras included mugs, soap dishes, slop jars and covers, water jugs, brush vases and trays.

Significant design energy was directed at these goods resulting in several new shapes and/or patterns being introduced each year. Quickly recognised as a particular strength of the firm, toilet sets were available to satisfy every conceivable customer requirement and price range. A choice of oval and round basins was offered together with various sizes of ewers encompassing simple plain forms to elaborate embossed details. Decorations ranged from inexpensive lithographic transfer border designs to handpainted patterns with gilt finishes.

A policy of progressive improvement in both the earthenware body and the applied decorations was coupled with an attention to detail that often drew favourable comments from the trade press. A typical example is the following report in the Pottery Gazette of April 1883 :

> *The Windsor shape, printed with a bold rich-looking design in English fruit, looks very effective. The same shape is also neatly decorated with an embossed tropical plant, care being taken in the arrangement so that it can easily be kept free from dirt getting into the embossed parts.*

Many shapes and patterns were designed specifically for toilet wares. However, these articles were also incorporated into the en-suite ranges such as Fluted and Louis, thereby providing an added variety. One particular byproduct of this approach, worthy of note, was the availability of matching toilet and trinket sets.

By the end of the First World War, sales of toilet wares had started to decline as more houses were being constructed with bathrooms. However, Fielding's managed to successfully prolong their production of these wares into the 1930's by utilising decorations, such as Birch and Mavis, that allowed the sets to be promoted as ornamental rather than useful articles. During these later years, the new patterns were generally applied to existing shapes such as DUNDEE and LEO which were first introduced in 1909 and 1911 respectively. Thus, the company was able to maintain its reputation for new styles without incurring the expense of new shape moulds for a product line which was known to have a limited future.

Although toilet ware ranges diminished in popularity, there was one article which continued to be made until the mid-1960's. Chamber pots were placed in an outer circle around the base of the bottle oven to absorb heat helping to prevent damage to the other wares. Hence, all potteries produced chamber pots everytime the kiln was fired and competitive pricing was required in order to achieve sales. The practice came to an end with the introduction of the Litherland kiln in 1963.

Ivrine figures of a Classical Figure, John Bull, Elephant and Dancing Girl, 1919.

Figures

Figure models were another area in which a thoroughness of approach combined with an enterprising attitude enabled the Devon Pottery to compete successfully with the continental manufacturers.

Ivrine and Bronzine

The first major foray into this field was with a series called Ivrine. Introduced at the British Industries Fair in 1919, the series initially comprised twenty-six models encompassing a mixture of statuesque, animal and bird figures. These competed directly with the type of figures in which the Austrian potteries had previously specialised. They made an immediate impact with orders being placed by many European buyers at the fair. The Pottery and Glass Record reviewed the range enthusiastically :

> *A classic subject, that of the female water carrier, was well modelled, both as regards form and draperies. .... there is movement in the dancing girl; strength in the elephant. .... refinement is embodied in the treatment and modelling of the undraped figure. John Bull illustrates life and energy.*

It is known that additions were made to the series including an owl, eagle, tiger and wolf. However, the entry in the pattern book was not updated. In particular, a variation called Bronzine was shown at the British Industries Fair in 1921. As their names suggest, the Ivrine and Bronzine ranges both drew their inspiration from, and indeed emulated, statuary traditionally made from ivory and bronze.

A number of naturalistically painted bird models were also introduced during 1921 and 1922. These included a kingfisher and a redcap, depicted in various attitudes such as in flight or perched, and were produced in two sizes.

Finally from this period, a figure of a footballer was shown at the British Industries fair in 1920. This was reported as being finely modelled and, it was thought, would have appeal to all lovers of the sport.

Art Deco

The demand for the figures produced by such continental factories as Goldscheider and Katzhutte was an opportunity not to be missed. Hence, the major design campaigns of the Thirties featured a significant number of these figures portraying ladies in stylish dress and poses.

First introduced in 1931, the figures were carefully modelled and well-decorated, many being the work of Kathleen Parsons and Walter Lamonby. Whilst such figures were relatively expensive, detailed market research again ensured that they were offered for sale at less than the equivalent imported models.

A selection of figures including the small nursery figures to the foreground.

From the range of matt glazed nude figures, 1937.

The Pottery and Glass Record commented :

Two of the most ambitious efforts we saw were beautifully modelled. Standing about 16inches high, one was a figure of a Dancing Lady in natural pose with shawl drapery in various colours. The other was also a female figure, entitled Beach Pyjamas - an equally charming effort.

Kathleen Parsons was also primarily responsible for a series of smaller size models, marketed under the name of Sutherland Figures. Initially made in the conventional manner, i.e. handpainted and glazed, a less expensive alternative was subsequently made available. The cost of these were reduced by having a single firing and then spraying with cellulose directly onto the biscuit ware, the decoration being undertaken by Fielding's subsidiary company, the Era Art Pottery. This cheaper technique resulted in a less durable product which is demonstrated by the poor condition of many of the surviving examples.

New models were periodically added to the range. In particular, at the British Industries Fair in 1937, a series of classically posed nude figures was introduced. Finished in pastel matt shaded glazes of green, ivory and white, these models were also available fully coloured.

Former Crown Devon employees recall a German lady who produced designs for figures in the late 1930's including a Peasant Girl model. It is highly probable that this was Greta Marks.

Some figures, such as Ki-Ki, were produced in both small and large sizes. In addition, the use of different colour treatments created a comprehensive selection from one mould. Further variety was achieved by offering many of the figures fitted as table lamps or with a mirror backdrop.

A key factor in the popularity of the figures was their suitability as gifts, an aspect which was given considerable prominence in advertisements and promotional litera-ture. To re-inforce and support this marketing approach, each figure was packaged in an appropriately fancy box.

However, it was primarily the element of fantasy, and sometimes pertness, in the dance subjects together with the fine character studies undertaken in the modern style which gave the figures such a strong appeal. The resulting success of the various ranges ensured their continued production throughout the Thirties. Many of the models were also produced after World War II although the cellulose Sutherland figures were discontinued circa 1940.

Children and Animals

Advertisements in the trade press of the mid to late Thirties highlight the availability of a range of small nursery figures. The series, of four models, portrayed babies and toddlers in various attitudes such as playing and sleeping, with the names SLEEPY BOY, PAULINE, DAVID and TONY. Unfortunately no further information has been found. However, this type of model became increasingly popular at this time and were manufactured by a number of potteries, most notably the Mabel Lucie Attwell Child Studies produced by Shelley.

In contrast to the graceful female figures, Fielding's also produced a number of animal models during the Thirties. For the Christmas trade of 1934, four interesting styles of weighted doorstops were introduced, modelled and decorated to depict a rabbit, dog, puppy and mouse. In 1935, the PERKY PUP series of nursery figures was launched to be augmented the following year by the KITTYCAT range. Both of these were available in assorted matt glaze colours and five model sizes. The larger ones could be utilised as doorstops whilst the smaller size was also available modified for use as money boxes or cruets. Other animal figures were produced during the 1930's such as a seated elephant balancing a yellow ball on his trunk.

Early 1941 witnessed the introduction of a new series of animal and bird 'grotesque' figures. Comprised of eight original models, these were offered in four different colour schemes - green, red or off-white with a black base, and black with a red base. A special feature was the elongated and narrow bases specially designed to fit the modern narrow mantlepiece. Although produced well into the 1950's, it is likely that this range only became available to the home market following the lifting of war-time restrictions.

A model of a Scotch Terrier was also introduced in the early Forties. This was offered in three colourways - black, white with black eyes and nose, and Brindle. This last alternative should have been the most expensive involving, as it did, three firings to achieve the desired effect. However, the pattern book indicates that the final painting was to be undertaken by the apprentice painters and perhaps this helped to reduce the final cost.

It is known that further models were periodically introduced but unfortunately few details are available. However, one example is the black and white panda which was launched in the 1960's in response to the interest generated by the Chinese pandas, An-An and Chi-Chi.

Wall Ornaments

The company specialised in a variety of wall ornaments in the late Thirties, some of which were based on natural subjects such as a squirrel and a fish.

One series for children depicted popular nursery rhyme and fairy story characters such as MOTHER GOOSE, LITTLE RED RIDING HOOD, HANSEL and GRETEL, PETER PIEMAN, MARY MARY QUITE CONTRARY and CINDERELLA.

A series of CHAMPION DOG head studies of the leading breeds was introduced circa 1938. These had the approval of a leading Kennel Club judge and were heavily marketed as ideal gifts for dog lovers with advertisements featuring the ornament alongside a picture of the dog on which it was based.

The series of wall ornaments, introduced in 1941.

The Grotesque range of figures, introduced in 1941.

Model	Champion Dog
202	Toydom. Man Zee
203	Wolstanton Bridgeen
204	Exquisite Model of Ware
205	Heather Realisation
206	Basford Revival
207	Modiste of Wolf Glen
211	Crackley Supreme Again
214	George of The River

A change of style was witnessed in 1941 with the launch of a series of six highly stylised figure models, several portraying characters in national costume. These included a Swiss hiker, a Dutch girl and a Spanish dancer. They were produced until the late 1950's but, as with the grotesque figures, were probably only available on the home market after 1952.

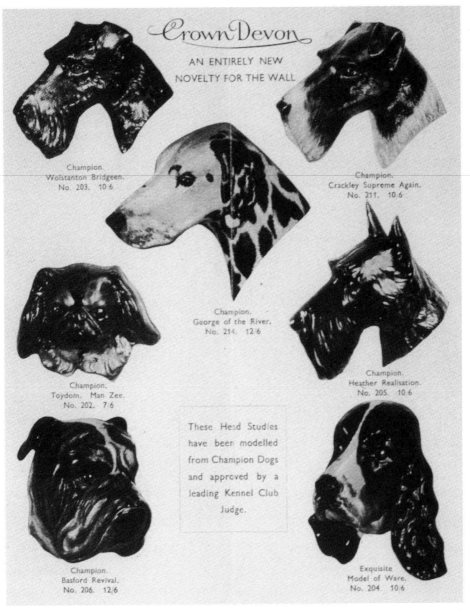

Champion Dog wall ornaments, introduced 1938.

Two extracts from a sales brochure showing a selection of musical novelties.

Musical Novelties

The Devon Pottery was a pioneer of home-produced musical earthenware novelties and was highly successful in both the home and export markets. Derived from the musical jugs and steins originating in Central Europe, these wares were embossed and handpainted with scenes and characters to complement the tunes played. A printed verse from the tune was incorporated into each decoration.

The musical movements were imported from three Swiss suppliers - Thorens SA, Al Reuge & Co., and Adrian Lador. Accounts were settled directly in Swiss Francs.

The cornerstone to the series was the JOHN PEEL design which was launched in 1930 and initially applied only to a jug and mug. However, its popularity was sustained and enhanced in the following years as the range of articles available was progressively extended to include such items as a plaque, loving cup, ashtray, flagon, cigarette box and even, a salad bowl with servers.

It was not until 1935 that two new decorations were added to the series, namely AULD LANG SYNE and WIDECOMBE FAIR. Welcome publicity was gained from an unexpected source when Sir Harry Lauder received an anonymous gift of an Auld Lang Syne musical jug during a visit to the Theatre Royal, Hanley. It prompted him to visit the factory where he was reported to be 'tickled to death' by the range of novelties available. Three years later, he was the inspiration for a musical jug, the brown handle of which was formed as his walking stick.

The range was strengthened during the following year (1936) by four further models - ILKLA MOOR, launched at the British Industries Fair in February with DAISY BELL, THE ASHGROVE and KILLARNEY presented later in the year in readiness for the Christmas trade.

In order to assist retailers to make a prominent and effective window display of the musical novelties, a special display stand was devised and made available on loan for a specified, limited period. These stands, constructed of three-ply with chromium pillars and alcoves, were provided fully fitted for electric lighting and ready for immediate use.

The British Industries Fair of 1937 was again the vehicle for the launch of new products. One was an adaptation of the Rio Rita figurine which revolved to the tune of The Merry Widow. In addition, a musical cigarette box modelled as a dog kennel was introduced. This had a detachable roof and was occupied by a black and white terrier. Activated by a lever, the tune 'Daddy Wouldn't Buy Me a Bow-Wow' played whilst the dog delivered the cigarette. Although something of a divergence from the style previously adopted for the range, they also met with success. The cigarette box received royal approval when Queen Elizabeth purchased one together with a Daisy Bell musical jug. The jug appears to have been a gift for the two princesses for, in a newspaper article of January 1946, Princess Elizabeth commented that it was still amongst their treasured possessions in the nursery.

In July 1937, a further innovative jug was introduced, designed by Violet Hayes and called THE ETON BOATING SONG. It featured a portrayal of an Eton boy as the handle whilst the embossed modelling on one side of the jug depicted the school boat crew in action against a background of Windsor Castle. The reverse side showed the college quadrangle complete with the Founder's statue. In describing this new production, the Pottery Gazette commented that :

> .... it's purpose is at once self-explanatory. The idea is that such a jug should serve as a memento to old Etonians of their schooldays and to this end everything that is incidental to the jug is Eton in spirit.

An interesting anecdote relating to this jug is that Queen Mary commanded the designer to forward one to her and the firm received notification a short time later of royal acceptance and approval.

The targeted marketing approach demonstrated by the Eton jug was developed further in a series of musical tankards for Cambridge, Oxford and Queen's University, Belfast. Each tankard had the university badge printed in black on the front with a deep band of the appropriate university colour to the foot. The reverse side was identical in all cases and comprised a verse of Auld Lang Syne printed in gold with an interlocking hands motif. The design was completed by gold lines on the handle and above the colour band at the base.

The coronation of George VI also took place in 1937, following the abdication of his brother, Edward VIII. As might be expected, musical commemoratives were a significant feature of the Fielding range. (A full description of these wares may be found in the section on commemoratives).

Musical novelties had been an overwhelming success story for the company during the 1930's and this was acknowledged in a trade report of early 1938 :

> Nowadays it is possible to encounter these lines almost everywhere, and it is not necessary to investigate very far to satisfy oneself that a good trade is being done with them.

However, not content to rest on their laurels, three new designs were added to the range based on popular stars of the day, namely Harry Lauder, the comedian Sandy Powell and Gracie Fields. The latter showed a street scene with Gracie singing Sally in Our Alley to the accompaniment of a barrel organ on the front. The reverse side incorporated a picture of Gracie Fields whilst the handle was modelled as an old-fashioned street lamp. Each jug also carried a reproduction of her signature, by special arrangement. Unsurprisingly, the tune was 'Sally in our Alley'.

The company had fostered close links overseas which had resulted in their strong export market position. Reginald Fielding, in particular, undertook many business tours and these were often the catalyst for specialised additions to the range of musical novelties. For example, the SARIE MARIAS musical jug was created to co-incide with his successful trip to South Africa in 1935. This depicted typical veldt scenes in relief modelling whilst the tune was a popular Boer song. General Smuts, Prime Minister of South Africa, sent a letter of congratulations after seeing the jug and, some years later in 1943, he was presented with a jug and tankard by Ross Fielding.

Similarly, the New Zealand HAERA-RA and Australian ADVANCE AUSTRALIA FAIR jugs were probably initiated by Reginald's tour of these countries in 1937, making their appearance in 1938. The Australian jug depicted Captain Cook landing amongst hostile natives with the handle being modelled as a kangaroo whilst the New Zealand jug portrayed a Maori scene. Another country related design was for a Bermuda musical jug although this was produced in more limited quantities.

A nurseryware series of miniature musical tankards was produced. These were transfer printed and did not have embossed details. Little information is available on the individual designs. However, two known patterns are LITTLE RED RIDING HOOD which played the tune of 'Who's afraid of the big bad wolf', and HUSH A BYE BABY.

The range of musical novelties also included chamber pots, of which two designs have been identified. The first has an illustration of a pub scene showing the landlord serving two customers at the bar. The tune was 'Oh landlord fill the flowing bowl'. The second pattern featured a bedroom scene showing the husband in bed and his wife leaving the room with a lighted candle. The tune was, appropriately enough, 'In the still of the night'.

For many years, considerable care and attention had been given to maximising seasonal trade, primarily in relation to Christmas. Even in the face of a major war, 1939 was no exception with the introduction of a musical cigarette box in the shape of a baby grand piano. Decorated in a cream matt glaze and finished in best burnished gold, the piano played a tune when the lid was lifted to reveal the cigarettes stored inside.

The introduction of government restrictions on decorated wares together with the difficulty in obtaining the musical movements brought production to a halt for the remainder of the Second World War.

However, as early as December 1945, the company was again advertising its range of musical novelties including the three new designs of THERE'LL ALWAYS BE AN ENGLAND, RULE BRITANNIA and THE STAR SPANGLED BANNER featuring suitably patriotic decorations.

At about this time, new musical jugs were designed which featured OLD ENGLISH and HUNTING scenes. They were printed and painted underglaze with green shading to top and bottom.

A new series of musical mugs was also introduced which were available in a choice of four plain colours - green, turquoise, crimson and yellow. All had a silver band to the top and bottom together with silver decoration to the handle. A further design, illustrating GAY NINETIES scenes, was completed by black shading to the top, bottom and handle.

The continuing restrictions on decorated goods for the home market meant that sales efforts were targeted towards exports during the late 1940's and early 1950's. The ability to build on their pre-war reputation and contacts enabled the firm to achieve considerable success with the popularity of the musical range being an important factor.

Although not readily available in the UK, the range continued to attract public attention through its use for presentation purposes. Such occasions were well-established and were often prompted by the affinity of the Fielding family to sport in all its forms. Don Bradman, the Australian cricketer, had received one of the Advance Australia Fair jugs whilst at Nottingham during the last tour by the team in 1938. A jug of the same design was presented to Stanley Matthews in 1946, following a civic luncheon in his honour to mark his record of forty-four international appearances for England. Bruce Woodcock, the British European and British Empire Heavyweight Boxing Champion visited the works in 1949, whilst in Stoke to give a boxing exhibition. Being a Yorkshireman, he received a musical jug which appropriately played the tune, Ilkla Moor.

Cognisant of the changing market conditions, a new moderately priced range was introduced in 1956. Based on the traditional designs, these had simpler forms with less embossment although they continued to be handpainted. Two new subjects were included in this range, THE FARMER'S BOY and THE SAILOR'S FAREWELL, the latter being an adaptation of an earlier lustre decoration.

Musical novelties retained their popularity throughout the 1950's and were regularly featured on the company's stands at trade exhibitions until 1962.

Stanley Matthews during a visit to the Devon Pottery in 1946.

Toby and Character Jugs

The earliest reference to character jugs was entered in the pattern books in 1902 when three models, namely a monkey jug, an Irishman jug and and an Old Woman Toby jug, are mentioned. The last of these was colourfully decorated by hand and had a green skirt, red bodice, white apron, fawn hat and yellow cape.

Toby jugs did not feature again until 1924 when one model, in a series of four colourways, was introduced. These appear to have been an inexpensive range since they required only one firing and had no finish to edges and handles. The jugs were available in marbled blues, pink, green and, yellow and brown.

The 1930's through to the late 1950's was the heyday of the musical novelties. These can be viewed as a variation of the character jug, particularly those inspired by the popular stars of the day. It seems likely that the success of the musical ranges precluded any further development of the standard Toby and character jugs during this period.

Character jugs were a well-established and popular product line of Shorter and Sons. It is not surprising, therefore, that their production was continued following the take-over by Fielding's in 1964, particularly as the musical ranges were being phased out by this time due to declining popularity. However, the range was rationalised to fourteen models together with three sizes of Toby teapot and a Toby mug complete with black lid. During the initial transition period, the articles often carried both the Shorter and Crown Devon backstamps. However, by the end of the 1960's, all Toby and character jugs were issued with only the Crown Devon mark.

The jugs were handpainted under-glaze and dipped in a straw glaze. They were available in three sizes, the size and model name being impressed on the base of each item.

The fourteen models of the series were :-

Beefeater	Long John Silver	Pensioner
Cavalier	Neptune	Scottie
Dick Turpin	Neptune (small)	Sheik
Guardsman	Parson John	Toby
Hayseed	Pedro	

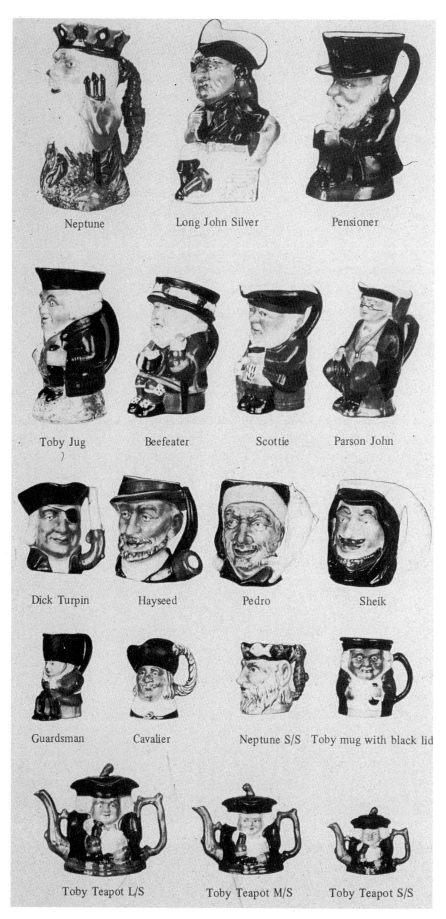

Neptune Long John Silver Pensioner

Toby Jug Beefeater Scottie Parson John

Dick Turpin Hayseed Pedro Sheik

Guardsman Cavalier Neptune S/S Toby mug with black lid

Toby Teapot L/S Toby Teapot M/S Toby Teapot S/S

The Crown Devon range of character and toby jugs, 1970's.

Nurserywares

Nurserywares were not given any particular prominence by Fielding's in their advertising and there are few reports in the trade press on these ranges.

The first recorded instance of Fielding's producing nurserywares was at the turn of the century (1900 - 1902) when lithographs of Kate Greenaway figure subjects were used. A series of baby's plates was produced between 1904 and 1910 which depicted subjects such as horses, cats, puppy and ducks, a maypole, hunting scenes, and teddy bears. Although the information available is incomplete, it is known that some of these patterns were applied utilising a background transfer print enhanced by handpainted enamels.

At the British Industries Fair, in 1917, the stand featured a good display of four-piece boxed toy teasets in several decorations. Three years later at the same venue, a new design in children's plates was introduced, prompting the Pottery Gazette to comment that they had a :

> .... sunk centre which prevents the food being scattered and meet a long felt want in the nursery and dining room.

No further references to nurserywares appear in the pattern books until the early 1930's when sets were produced which comprised items such as a soup bowl, a 7" plate, a cruet, a small jug and a covered handled beaker. Patterns included fairies, assorted animals (ZOO series) and characters from nursery rhymes such as Tommy Tucker, Boy Blue, Curly Locks and Little Miss Muffet. Representations of nursery rhymes also formed the basis of a further series in the late 1930's and early 1940's, for example the Cat and the Fiddle, Ride-a-Cock-Horse and Little Bo-Peep. All of these were predominately lithographic transfer designs with a handpainted finish to edges and handles, on either yellow or ivory glazes.

Towards the end of the Thirties, permission was sought and granted by Walt Disney to produce small figurines of Mickey and Minnie Mouse. However, only a small quantity were ever produced. It should be noted that nurserywares of the Thirties also encompassed wall ornaments and figures, such as the Perky Pup range, which are described in more detail in the section on figures. However, these products do highlight the particular suitability of nurserywares as gifts. An aspect which was re-inforced again with the promotion of 'Gifts For Children' in displays at the Blackpool Fairs of 1957 and 1958. The Pottery Gazette of March 1958 reported that :

> There were also some potentially quick-selling money boxes at this stand, including the ubiquitous Sooty.

It is clear that nurserywares continued to form a small but significant part of the company's production. The last known reference being to the CHICKADEE set in 1979. This was presented in its own giftbox (which doubled as a display carton) and contained a small plate, cereal bowl, mug and eggcup.

Clocks and Lamps

It is known that clock cases were produced by Fielding's at the turn of the century until at least 1910. From anecdotal evidence, there were a number of different shaped cases decorated with a variety of designs including several of the Royal series and flow-blue patterns. However, there is very little documentary material concerning these products.

Clocks rarely featured in the firm's publicity, indeed the only known example appeared in the Pottery Gazette in 1898 as part of a composite advertisement illustration. Interestingly, this showed a clock case only, i.e. without the clock movement fitted. The only other reference from this period appears in 1910. This was also in the Pottery Gazette which reported that Fielding's had many pieces well-suited for presents including clock sets described as *exceedingly neat*.

Clocks were produced during the 1930's but again, few details are available. However, it is recorded that wall clock sets fitted with English movements were shown at the British Industries Fair in 1939.

Finally, wall clocks are known from the post-war period, particularly the 1960's.

Fortunately, there are more details concerning the lamp ranges. These were introduced in the early 1930's and were generally supplied with matching hand painted celluloid shades.

Lamps were available to match many of the ornamental decorations, for example the Orient modernist and the Mattajade Dragon patterns. However, there were also several decorations designed specifically for lamps. These included shaded bands of varying depths, handcraft floral motifs and, scrolls with lines and dots. Lamps were often shown at the British Industries Fairs and received favourable comments, as in 1936 when the Pottery and Glass Record reported :

> *Some good modern types of lamp standards seen in a variety of decorations, effective in line and purpose.*

Other lamp bases at this time were the John Peel and Hunting models. The John Peel lamp was an extension to the popular range of wares in this design, many of which were fitted with musical movements. The pattern book indicates that it was to be under-glaze printed and then painted by Walter Lamonby. The Hunting lamp was moulded in the form of a tree with fox hounds at its base and was also handpainted under-glaze.

The attractive figure models of the 1930's were offered pierced and fitted up as table lamps. These had chromium plated backs and silk shades which harmonised with the colourings of each model.

The range was not confined to table lamps with some hanging wall lamps also being produced. Two of these were shown at the British Industries Fair in 1938, one of which was described in the Pottery and Glass Record, as follows :

Notably pleasing, a representation of a Spanish balcony with figures in pink and a flowered canopy done in fawn and pink shades relieved with green on a grey mottled ground.

A series of simply decorated lamp bases was introduced in the early 1940's. These were decorated in green, blue, yellow or pink glazes and, except for the yellow version, were embellished with gold lines.

Following the war, the majority of lamps were supplied as bases only, without the matching shades of the 1930's. This facilitated a higher level of production and enabled the company to supply a number of specialist lighting firms including Elliott and Spears, The Electric Art Company and, Alladin's.

In the 1950's, lamps were again produced to complement other ornamental wares. One example was the embossed stag and trees design which was available in the three colourways of brown, green and, blue with yellow. Others featured sgraffito decoration or fluted shapes whilst the carved tulips pattern incorporated the treacle glaze popular at this time.

Novelty was also evident, particularly in a television lamp in the form of a crinoline lady which apparently caught the attention of several buyers at the Blackpool Fair in 1956.

Giftware

Fielding's was well aware of the sales potential of giftwares and many of the ornamental and tableware products were promoted as such. However, from an early stage, certain articles were designed primarily as gifts and these usually incorporated a novelty element to add to their appeal.

Although ladies were always well-catered for, a particularly delightful novelty range was introduced in 1910. These were eggs which could be used as hair tidies, pin boxes or similar as well as being highly decorative. The first series of designs featured plain 'solid' silver or gold, a forget-me-not lithograph and, a goose print and enamel pattern. The eggs were also used as commemoratives for the coronation of George V. A further series of designs was introduced in 1914 which included animal and bird subjects, and Cinderella characters, all of which were lithographs. A more expensive decoration featured a horseshoe printed in gold with a forget-me-not lithograph applied over it and the whole finished in gold.

With the aim of providing novelties suitable as gifts for men, a range of tobacco jars was introduced in 1902. These had a vellum background and one popular pattern featured a pheasant and partridge. In addition, and perhaps influenced by Abraham Fielding's love of all sporting activities, other decorations depicted golf, cricket and football subjects. It is interesting to note that these designs were modified within two months of their entry into the pattern books to incorporate trees between the players. Tobacco jars were also used as commemoratives for the coronation of Edward VII in 1902.

The air-tight properties of the jars generated particular interest in the trade press as evidenced by the following explanatory report from the Pottery Gazette :

> *The cover has a double-screw metal fitting. On the underside of the outer edge of the cover there is a rubber band which fits into a groove at the top of the jar but in such a position that it cannot possibly come into contact with the contents of the jar. The jar has an ordinary lock-lid arrangement but, in addition, there is a metal screw which presses the lid firmly down and the rubber band renders the jar absolutely airtight.*

Tobacco jars next appear in the pattern books in the early 1930's when a series of five decorations were entered. These relied on colour for their effect, featuring either groundlaid or stippled backgrounds in predominantly dark tones. All were finished with a gold knob and edge. A further design showing hunting scenes and finished in gold was introduced in approximately 1934.

Another range appealing to masculine interests was introduced in 1939/40. This comprised straw glaze mugs with six printed designs on a drinking theme. The subjects were a Cavalier, Francis Drake, a Dicken's character, a Farmer, a Town Crier and a Coachman.

A nostalgic element was evident in the moustache cups introduced in 1967. Purely decorative in function, the patterns included Coaching Scenes and The Sailor's Farewell.

An interesting range of photographic products was introduced in the 1970's. These enabled customers to combine a photograph with the article of their choice using a laminated photographic process. Initially, a series of embossed border plates of various sizes was available. However, the range was subsequently extended to include a mug, round puff box, cowbell, round money box, cigarette box and miniature skillet.

Finally, pets were not forgotten with the introduction of the Supreme range of Animal Feeding Dishes in the 1970's. Three designs were available entitled WALKIES, DOG-TAG, and PURR-FECTION, the first of which was offered in two sizes. The dishes were sold in special individual packaging and marketed under the slogan '*Supreme dogs and cats dine off Supreme dishes'*.

Sizes & capacities (Metric).

WALKIES......
M/S (18cm.)   1.28 litres
S/S (16cm.)   0.85 litres

DOG...TAG...
M/S (18cm.)   1.28 litres
S/S (16cm.)   0.85 litres

PURR.....FECTION
S/S (13cm.)   0.43 litres

The Supreme range of pet dishes, 1970's.

Souvenir Ware

Souvenir ware had first become popular after World War I when a greater emphasis on travel coupled with a sense of community pride led hundreds of towns to want mementos for visitors and residents. Although many potteries produced these miniature ornaments, most notably W.H. Goss, there is no evidence that Fielding's competed in this market at this time.

Typical English scenes had formed the basis of Crown Devon designs from the turn of the century but these cannot be classified as 'true' souvenir ware. It is not until the mid-1930's that the first examples appeared. Arguably, the first such pattern was a scene of Cockington Forge applied to cider mugs which was handpainted under a brown glaze and finished in silver. However, it is the two designs for the Isle of Wight that display all the essential characteristics of souvenirs. One depicts gnomes playing cards around a toadstool table with the inscription '2B Gamblers All, Ye Ancient Smugglers of Blackgang Chine, IOW'. The second incorporates a view of Blackgang Chine and has the words 'Blackgang Chine and The Needles, IOW'. Both patterns were applied using the print and enamel method against a straw glaze background and were available on a range of suite ware.

Further decorations were produced for holiday destinations including the Gorleston and Butlin's Skegness holiday camps, Guernsey and Rhyl. Suitable mottos were often applied, such as 'Happy Memories of Guernsey' and 'Fragrant Memories of Rhyl'. Again, a range of articles was available from complete coffee sets to a boxed sweet dish.

With the outbreak of war, attention was generally turned to export markets and the souvenir trade sector was no exception. Hence, the 1940's saw the introduction of many designs specifically targeted at the American, Canadian, Australian and New Zealand markets. These typically featured scenes of the respective country, particular buildings of interest or illustrations of historical events. Examples include the Canadian Scenes series, the Australian Exhibition Buildings series and the New Zealand Captain Cook series.

It is interesting to note that, prior to World War II, souvenir ware was sold by the company's travelling sales representatives as part of the overall range of wares. However, a change of policy in the post-war years resulted in the appointment of an agent, the Wynstay Manufacturing Company. Hence, all orders and consequent distribution for the home market was channelled through this agent who increasingly participated in design decisions concerning the range.

Souvenir ware was produced until the 1950's when demand diminished.

Art Deco figures. It is interesting to note the similarity between the Goldscheider figure (far left) and the corresponding Crown Devon figure alongside it.

Animal figures including Perky Pups (centre) and a panda from the 1960's.

Wall ornaments, this range was introduced in 1941.

JOHN PEEL FLAGON
25 /-
Height 7½"

JOHN PEEL JUG
23 /6
Height 7½"

AULD LANG SYNE
½-Pint Tankard
15 /9

AULD LANG SYNE JUG
23 /6
Height 7½"

JOHN PEEL
1-Pint Tankard
19 /6

WIDDICOMBE FAIR
1-Pint Tankard
21 /-

ILKLA MOOR JUG
23 /6
Height 8"

WIDDICOMBE FAIR
½-Pint Tankard
17 /6

WIDDICOMBE FAIR JUG
24 /6
Height 8"

JUG AND TWO TANKARDS IN EACH SERIES

Page from a sales brochure showing a selection of musical novelties.

171

Eton Boating Song musical tankard.

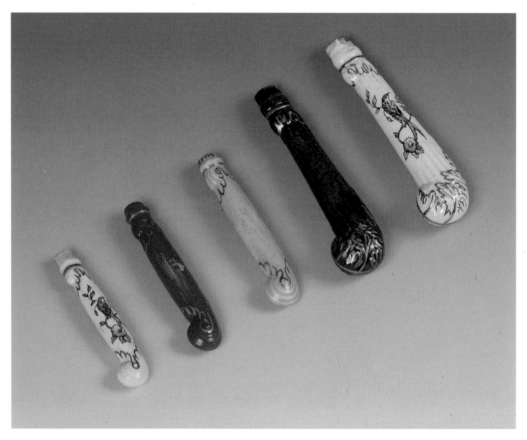

A range of knife handles, date unknown.

Character jugs and toby teapots; Neptune (top left), Pirate (top right), Guardsman (centre left), Beefeater (centre) and Sheik (bottom left). The toby jug (top centre) is an early example probably dating from the early 1900's.

A selection of nurserywares including a toy teaset from circa 1917, a cruet from the 1930's, and a post-war money box.

The Chickadee nurseryware range of the 1970's.

Souvenir wares.

A selection of tablewares from a special set; this pattern was not put into general production.

Commemoratives

Significant events in the nation's history, especially those connected with the reigning monarch, were usually commemorated by the issue of specially decorated items. The ceramics industry, in particular, viewed such occasions as a welcome boost to their normal sales and S. Fielding & Co. was no exception to this general rule. They enthusiastically produced comprehensive ranges of wares, usually with at least one item of novelty appeal.

Victoria

Victoria had distanced herself and family from the public following the death of Prince Albert. As a result, the Silver Jubilee of her reign had not been celebrated nor had her declaration as Empress of India in 1877. She had undertaken few state visits and royal weddings had been essentially family affairs. The British people, therefore, had been starved of events to celebrate.

Hence, it was with some uncertainty that the pottery manufacturers approached Victoria's Golden Jubilee in 1887; most of the commemoratives produced were relatively crude with a predominance of transfer printed decorations. However, following the success of 1887, vast quantities of commemoratives were produced for the Diamond Jubilee in 1897. The designs were generally more ornate and the use of photographic portraits was widespread.

No record has been found of any commemoratives being issued by Fielding's for either event. However, given the general background, it is difficult to believe that a man with Abraham Fielding's keen commercial sense would have failed to take advantage of these opportunities.

Boer War (1899 - 1902)

The first known commemoratives issued by Fielding's were produced in 1900 and related to the Boer War.

The war had started in 1899 and, initially, the Boers had considerable success with British garrisons besieged at Ladysmith, Mafeking and Kimberley. However, between February and August 1900, British counter-offensives under Lord Roberts led to the relief of the garrisons and the occupation of the Boer capital, Pretoria. Hence, the commemoratives were produced at a time of British successes after the preceding period of unimaginable defeats.

There were two main designs, with several variations, applied to a range of articles including Oban and Louis shape suite ware. The first design featured a Coat of Arms and a five flag emblem whilst the second was a photographic lithograph of the generals involved.

Edward VII and Alexandra (1901 - 1910)

Edward VII became king in his 60th year and although he had widespread popularity, there were many who doubted his ability to take over the reins of power and maintain the

Commemorative wares including a Spitfire wall plaque (centre left) with 'Hitler'
ashtray in front, and Edward VIII abdication mug (top right).

stability of the monarchy. However, he worked hard at his task during his brief reign and was admired both at home and abroad, with his epithet of 'Peacemaker' being well-deserved.

It is interesting to note that the coronation ceremony had to be postponed at the last minute, from June 26th to August 9th 1902, because the King had to undergo an emergency operation for appendicitus. Obviously, by the time of the postponement, a large number of commemorative items had already been issued and it is, therefore, not unusual to find pieces which have an incorrect date.

Fielding's produced a large number of interesting coronation souvenirs including flowerpots and dessert services together with both earthenware and china mugs. The decorations featured lithographic portraits of the king and queen, some being further embellished with a rose, shamrock and thistle spray. Flags of Empire were also added in some instances. The novelty item was a perfectly air-tight tobacco jar which was particularly well-suited for presentation purposes.

The king's death in 1910 was also the occasion for a range of commemoratives, although a smaller number were produced. One such item was a two-handled loving cup, decorated with a simple but effective black transfer showing a framed portrait of Edward. This in turn was partially framed with a leaf design and the inscription : "In Memoriam. Edward The Peacemaker. King and Emporer". The reverse side recorded the dates of his birth, marriage, coronation and death. The rim and handles were finished with thin silver bands.

George V and Mary (1910 - 1936)

George V came to the throne during difficult times both at home and abroad. However, he was assured of public affection because of the esteem in which his father had been held.

A comprehensive range of useful and ornamental goods was produced featuring a new and registered design, exclusive to Fielding's, which was very carefully executed. As might be expected, the design included portraits of the royal couple together with regal emblems. Once again, an interesting novelty item was offered. In this instance, it was 'Easter Eggs' with brightly enamelled coronation decorations. The eggs were adaptable for use as ladies' hair tidies, pin boxes or similar purposes and, therefore, made excellent presents.

For the Silver Jubilee celebrations in 1935, a mug was available which highlighted the notable achievements of the reign and showed the Empire on two hemispheres. This very detailed and colourful design of a world map showed the British Empire in red with a number of historic events being commemorated. These included 'Queen Mary Launched', 'Royal Scot', 'American Tour', 'Sydney Harbour Bridge Built', and 'The First Wireless Broadcast'. The marriage and coronation dates were also included. The reverse side featured the royal arms and flags.

World War I (1914 - 1918)

With the outbreak of war, a number of articles decorated with a patriotic emblem lithograph were produced. Unfortunately, no further details are available.

However, it is known that a mug was issued to commemorate peace in 1919. The colourful front illustration depicted a seated Brittania surrounded by flags of all the nations involved. A globe above her head, circled by a banner declaring 'Peace', was surmounted by a hovering dove. Below her feet, a further banner carried the words 'Liberty, Justice, Truth, Honour'. The reverse side, printed in black, carried a shield overlaying crossed swords and sprays of thistles, roses and shamrock leaves. The inscription within the shield read : 'Sir David Beatty's Historic Signal. The German flag is to be hauled down at Sunset to-day, and is not to be hoisted again without permission. Nov. 21st 1918.' The dates of the declaration of war, the signing of the General Armistice and the signing of the Peace were given below the shield decoration. The edges and handle were finished in gold.

Edward VIII (1936)

The proposed coronation of Edward VIII inspired the firm to produce their largest and most elaborate range of commemoratives to date.

One series of designs, used on items such as beakers, had relief mouldings of the king's head to the front and crown to the reverse. The cream body, two thin red and blue lines on the base and an inscription in gold were the only colours giving the items a dramatic simplicity.

However, it was the adaptation of their popular musical wares which caught the imagination of the trade press and buying public alike. Mugs were made in three sizes (small, half-pint and one pint) which, together with a large size jug, were fitted with a musical movement set to play "God Save The King" when the item was lifted.

There was also a limited edition of 1500 of an extra large jug which stood some 14 inches tall. This was embossed at the front with the king's head framed within suitable heraldry whilst the reverse featured the king's herald with Balmoral and Windsor castles in the background. Each jug was accompanied by a parchment scroll which recorded its particular number within the edition. In previewing the launch of this 'super piece', the Pottery Gazette expected that the retail price would be in the region of four to five guineas, but commented that each jug was :

> A wonderful article, and one worthy of being prized and carefully preserved.

All items leaving the factory after the abdication announcement carried the words 'Abdicated December 10th 1936'. It is unlikely that musical movements were fitted to these articles.

George VI and Elizabeth (1936 - 1952)

George VI became king following the abdication of his elder brother, Edward VIII. In most cases, an identical range of commemorative items was produced for the new king as had been made for the proposed coronation of Edward VIII, with only the portraits and names being changed.

In particular, a new limited edition of 1500 of the large musical jugs was launched.

The only difference was the availability of an alternative tune, "Here's a Health Unto His Majesty" in addition to "God Save The King".

Commemoratives were also issued in association with important overseas visits such as the one to South Africa in 1947. These had a cream body and relief mouldings of the royal couple's heads to the front and a leaping springbok to the reverse.

There are no records of items commemorating the King's death.

World War II (1939 - 1945)

A number of products were 'inspired' by World War II and produced during the war years. One design for beakers featured the embossed heads and shoulders of a soldier, sailor and airman with the wording 'On To Victory' printed in old gold above. The decoration was completed by two thin lines in blue and red to the foot and a straw glaze background. Two versions were available, the more expensive of which had a gold edge and handle instead of the standard red finish.

A wall plaque commemorating the Battle of Britain received royal approval with the purchase of one by the Queen. The moulded plaque depicted a Spitfire speeding through the clouds and is inscribed with Winston Churchill's famous words 'Never was so much owed by so many to so few'.

The firm's novelty range of figures was extended in 1941 by the introduction of the JOHN BULL and BOMBARDIER doorstops, standing 7" and 10" high respectively. It is interesting to note that the John Bull model was quickly adapted, by the addition of a hat and cigar, into a Churchill commemorative.

Finally, musical chamber pots, decorated with a cartoon drawing of either Hitler or Mussolini, were produced. The rim had iron crosses and swastikas together with inscriptions such as 'Another violation of Poland' and 'Have this on Old Nasty'. A miniature version, for use as an ashtray, was also produced which had the revised inscription 'Flick your ash on Old Nasty'. This did not have a musical movement.

Elizabeth II (1952 -)

For the coronation in June 1953, the range of commemoratives was similar to those which had been produced for her father and uncle. In particular, a relief moulded design depicted the heads of the queen and Prince Phillip with a delicate tinting of the features. A straw glaze background and a minimum of other ornamentation completed the decoration. This was used for a series of articles such as beakers, tankards, ashtrays and cigarette boxes. The tankards and cigarette boxes could optionally be supplied with musical movements which played the National Anthem.

Unfortunately, few details of more recent commemoratives are available. However, it is known that a series of lidded two-handled loving cups was introduced for the Silver Jubilee in 1977. These were available in a choice of background colours including green

Novelty war-time commemoratives of the Bombardier, embossed Services beaker and Churchill as John Bull (left to right). Introduced in 1941/42.

Patriotic musical jugs, introduced in 1946/47.

and blue. Commemoratives were also produced for the wedding of Prince Charles and Lady Diana Spencer in 1981. Articles included plaques, loving cups and beakers which were decorated with lithographic transfer prints and were generally of a poor quality.

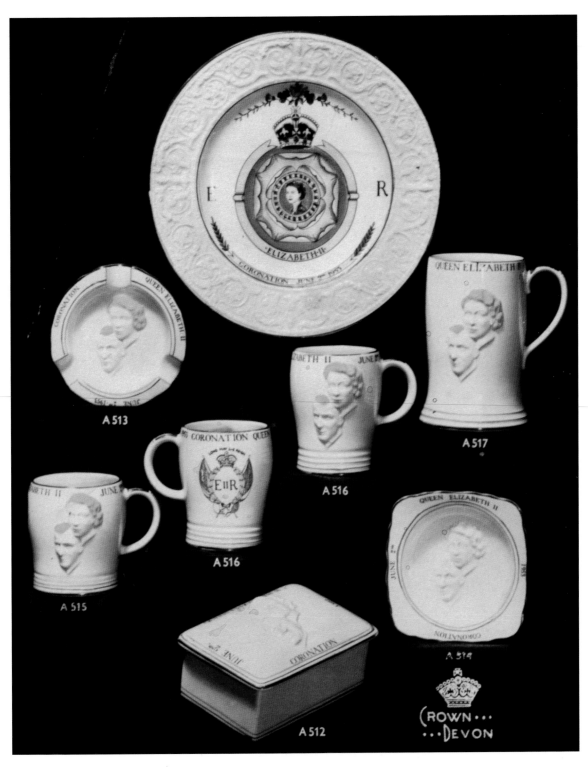

Advertising leaflet for Elizabeth II coronation commemoratives.

Commercial Customers

In addition to selling their own designs and product lines through wholesalers and retail shops, Fielding's supplied a range of other commercial customers. There were several aspects to this business including the supply of plain ware to other potteries for subsequent decoration by them; production of advertising articles; the supply of wares for commercial use or resale under the customer's name; and collaborative ventures with well-known retail organisations.

Plain Wares

Several potteries operated as decorating houses only and did not manufacture their own products preferring to purchase white wares from other factories. Fielding's was a supplier of such white wares to a number of potteries including A.E. Gray & Co Ltd.

In a similar manner, Fielding's supplied the Fulham Pottery with large plain white and black matt ornamental wares together with large water filters during the 1950's.

Advertising

The production of useful and ornamental articles for advertising and promotional purposes was a noted speciality of the firm. The earliest known examples are three designs for change plates for use on shop counters which were entered into the pattern books between 1907 and 1910. These promoted 'Standard Dark Flake', 'Robins Cigarettes', and 'Beeswing : 10 Cigarettes 2.5d'. They were transfer printed and had a single firing in order to keep costs to a minimum.

The range also included match-strikers, ash trays and jugs. They were well-received with the Pottery and Glass Record of 1915 stating :

> *They have achieved remarkable results so that we strongly advise dealers to inspect their samples before deciding to place orders elsewhere.*

A variation of this line was the production of 'badge' ware during the 1960's and 1970's such as plates for Lyons Tearooms and serving dishes for Quantas Airlines, each of which carried the customer's company name and/or logo.

Such product lines were featured regularly at trade fairs as well as forming part of the display in the London showroom.

Collaborative Ventures

From the 1950's onwards, Fielding's embarked on a number of collaborations with selected organisations, in particular Fortnum and Mason, and Oppenheimer.

The association with Fortnum and Mason began in the 1950's with the supply of caviar jars in various sizes. These were expensive to manufacture since they featured a solid base

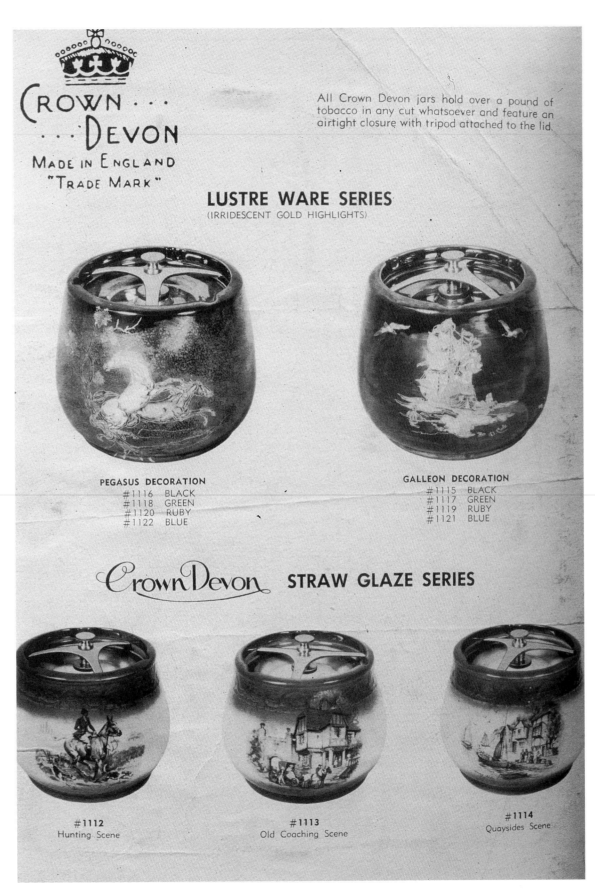

CROWN··· ···DEVON

MADE IN ENGLAND
"TRADE MARK"

All Crown Devon jars hold over a pound of tobacco in any cut whatsoever and feature an airtight closure with tripod attached to the lid.

LUSTRE WARE SERIES
(IRRIDESCENT GOLD HIGHLIGHTS)

PEGASUS DECORATION

#1116   BLACK
#1118   GREEN
#1120   RUBY
#1122   BLUE

GALLEON DECORATION

#1115   BLACK
#1117   GREEN
#1119   RUBY
#1121   BLUE

CrownDevon STRAW GLAZE SERIES

#1112
Hunting Scene

#1113
Old Coaching Scene

#1114
Quaysides Scene

A series of tobacco jars made for Oppenheimer & Co Ltd, mid 1960's.

of clay which, incidentally, also made them very heavy to handle. The pattern books record the design for a multi-coloured vase in the Italian style, in 1960. Four years later, a further entry indicates that a vase decorated with the Cedar Tree pattern printed under a pearl glaze was also supplied exclusively to the store.

However, it was in 1970 that Crown Devon became a major supplier of the ceramics which formed the basis for much of Fortnum and Mason's giftware. An extensive range of articles was involved including tureens, storage jars, ginger jars, caskets, trinket boxes, powder bowls, soap dishes, tankards and flowerpots. Some were incorporated into luxury hampers such as the casserole containing Stilton cheese and the hors d'oeuvres dish filled with hand-made chocolates for Christmas 1976. Others were sold as individual gifts filled with everything from crystallised cherries to soap, with stem ginger and 'pure exotic honey' being particular favourites. A comprehensive selection of patterns were utilised, the majority of which were standard Crown Devon designs, for example Pegasus, Lowestoft and Cries of London. The arrangement continued throughout the 1970's but no further orders appear to have been placed after November 1979.

An exclusive range of tobacco jars were produced in conjunction with A. Oppenheimer & Co Ltd from 1963. The jars held over a pound of tobacco in any cut and featured an airtight enclosure with tripod attachment. Several designs were available including a pheasant and woodcock pattern printed in gold on a matt black glaze with hand painted enamel embellishments. In contrast, there was also a simple hand painted crayon decoration finished in a choice of black, green or brown glaze. The lustre ware series comprised the Pegasus and Galleon patterns highlighted in iridescent gold and available in the four colourways of black, green, ruby and blue. Finally, there were three designs illustrating Hunting, Old Coaching, and Quayside scenes respectively, in the straw glaze series.

Several product lines were produced for other commercial customers including perfume bottles for the Aidee Perfumery Company and teapots for Goblin for use with their Teasmade ranges. An interesting aspect of the contract with Goblin was their condition that all substandard or 'seconds' wares had to be smashed rather than sold off cheaply as was more usual. Lidded casserole dishes or stew pots were made in two sizes for Green Shield Stamps. These were of a ridged shape and featured embossed patterns in several single, solid colourways.

A number of ranges were produced for the American company, Crownford, including the Christmas series designed by Cuthbertson. Crown Devon products were also featured in the catalogues of two other retailers during this period; a preserve pot in the shape of an orange and honeycomb honey box were sold by the General Trading Co. whilst the Charlotte pattern range was offered by the Inside Out Shop, part of the Covent Garden General Store. None of these items carried the Crown Devon backstamp.

Appendix A : Backstamps

The following backstamps provide a useful guide to dating. It should be noted that Fielding's produced their own backstamps and this may be the reason for the many variations found to each distinctive backstamp.

FIELDING

Impressed mark
c. 1879+
Used on a limited number of wares at various periods of the firm's production.

GAME COCK

The 'Ceramic Art of Great Britain' by Jewitt (1883) records this mark. No actual examples have been identified.

Printed mark
c. 1891 - 1913

Printed mark
c. 1891 - 1913
Variation :
- addition of pattern name below shield

Printed mark
c. 1900+
Variation :
- without pattern name

Printed mark
c. 1900+

Printed mark
c. 1903+

Printed mark
c. 1913+
Variations :
- 'S.F. & Co' replaced by 'FIELDING'
- addition of pattern name below mark
- addition of pattern name and registered number
  below mark

Printed mark
c.1917 - 1930

Printed mark
c. 1917 - 1930
Variations :
- 'ENGLAND' replaced by 'MADE IN ENGLAND'
- 'FIELDING'S' replaced by 'S.F. & Co'
- all text above crown with pattern name and/or
  registered number below crown
- addition of pattern name below mark

Printed mark
c. 1917 - 1930

Printed mark
c. 1917 - 1930

Printed marks
c. 1930 - 1965
Variations :
- addition of 'FIELDING'S' above 'MADE IN
  ENGLAND'
- 'MADE IN ENGLAND' replaced by 'ENGLAND'
- addition of 'Rd APPLIED FOR' below trade mark
- addition of pattern name above or below mark

CROWN DEVON
CRETIAN
FIELDING
STOKE ON TRENT.

Printed mark
c. 1930+

CROWN DEVON
DELPH
FIELDING
STOKE·ON·TRENT
ENGLAND

Hand painted mark
c. 1930+

CROWN ··
··DEVON
MADE IN
ENGLAND

Rubber-stamped mark
c. 1939+

Rubber-stamped mark
c. 1939+

Printed mark
c. 1940+

Printed mark
c. 1957+

Printed mark
c. 1964+

Printed mark
c. 1964+

Printed mark
c. 1968+

Printed mark
c. 1968+
Variation of previous mark, used on small items

Printed mark
c. 1968+
Variations :
- omission of 'EST. 1853'
- 'EST. 1853' replaced by 'Potters For Over 100 Years'
- 'EST. 1853' replaced by 'Potters For 150 Years'
- addition of pattern name below mark

Era Art Pottery (1930 - 1947)

Printed mark
c. 1930+

Printed mark
c. 1930+

Printed mark
c. 1936+

Era Ware MADE IN ENGLAND

Printed mark
c. 1936+

Era Art Pottery (1930 - 1947) continued

Printed mark
c. 1939+

Baifield Productions Ltd

Printed mark
c. 1964+

Royal Crownford

Printed mark
c.1965+
NOTE : Several manufacturers produced for
Crownford. Hence, items with this mark are not
necessarily Crown Devon.

Appendix B : The People

S. Fielding & Co was a family firm in more ways than one. The Fielding family founded and owned the business through four generations, building it into a major earthenware manufacturer. Abraham and Reginald Fielding, in particular, fostered a genuine team spirit in the workplace to which the staff readily responded.

The company was a popular employer to the extent that workers were prepared to accept lower wages in order to work there. Several past employees have commented that the pay was lower than some other potteries but that it was a very happy place at which to work.

The prevailing community atmosphere was re-inforced in several ways. The majority of the workforce lived in close proximity to the factory whilst any vacancies were often filled by friends or relatives of existing staff. The Lamonby family is a typical example. Walter Lamonby (senior) was the senior artist for many years and his four children all joined the firm in various roles. The eldest son, Walter, became biscuit warehouse manager at Crown Devon whilst his brother, Eric, became a manager at the associated company of C.J. Baines. The third son, Dennis, worked in the warehouse of the subsidiary Era Art Pottery prior to World War II during which he was killed in Africa. The only daughter, Phyllis, was employed as a paintress with Crown Devon.

Those who were not related before joining the pottery often changed their status during the course of their employment since marriages between the staff were frequent occurrences.

The company also had close links with two local schools, St Peters and Herons Cross, the latter being Abraham's old school. Many school leavers were recruited from these schools for junior positions at the factory. However, the association was closer than that of a local employer and potential workforce, as illustrated by two events. A new block at Heron's Cross was named after Abraham and for which he performed the opening ceremony shortly before his death in 1932. In November 1967, Reginald, as a Governor of the school, instituted the Abraham Fielding Cup. In presenting the cup which stood for achievement in work, achievement in play, honesty and integrity, Reginald told the assembly :

> *I had the highest regard for my grandfather, and have always wanted to commem-*
> *orate his name in some way*

It is obviously impossible to name all the staff who worked at the Devon Pottery. However, the following short profiles highlight some of the key figures whilst other well-remembered characters are also listed. The two extracts from the wages book provide a further insight into the people involved and the list of agents gives additional historical snapshots.

George Barker

Worked as a travelling representative for 24 years, being employed by Wiltshaw & Robinson (Carltonware) immediately prior to joining Crown Devon. Appointed Sales Director in 1930, he had a major influence on the design campaigns of that period. He was a Freemason and past Master of the Ceramic Lodge.

Enoch Boulton

Served his apprenticeship at Grimwade's whilst attending the Burslem School of Art, probably on a part-time basis. Subsequently moved to Wiltshaw & Robinson where he was initially employed as a designer and progressed to Decorating Manager.

'Enie', as he was affectionately known, joined Fielding's in late 1929 as Design and Decorating Manager, ultimately being appointed Art Director in September 1949. In these roles, he was responsible for many of the best selling wares of the period. Highly respected at Fielding's and within the industry generally, he was particularly close to Reginald Fielding and often accompanied him to trade events such as the Leipzig Fair.

He left the company in 1950 to become Commercial Director at Coalport China, joining Stanley Harrison with whom he had served during World War II. He stayed with Coalport until his retirement.

Away from work, he had a great love of football and became a Vice President of Stoke City Football Club, along with Ned Taylor and Hubert Beswick. With these companions, he attended all internationals and cup finals as well as the Stoke matches. His other sporting passion was golf which he played well becoming President of his local club. Other interests included opera and he was Chairman of the Stoke Operatic Society for many years.

A modest and gentle man, his death was widely mourned. The following extract, from Reginald Fielding's letter to his widow, encapsulates the prevailing sentiment of those that knew him :

> *As you probably know, I knew Enie for some 40 years and whilst we were together in business, never a cross word. I thought a lot of Enie and I think he had some thoughts for myself. I don't think he had an unkind thought for anyone.*

John Thomas Broome

Was with the firm from boyhood, a total of nearly 51 years of service. For many years, he had acted as receptionist at the factory in addition to having responsibility for all overseas orders. He was Commercial manager at the time of his death in March 1937, at the age of 64.

He was a talented singer with a rich tenor voice and, in his younger days, had taken the principal role in a number of Gilbert and Sullivan operas produced by the North

Staffordshire Operatic society. He had been a member of several church choirs and often took part in charity concerts. A Freemason and a past Master of the Sutherland Lodge of Unity, Newcastle, his services as a singer were much invoked and extolled in Masonic circles.

F.E. Goodwin

Joined the firm in 1901 and appointed a director in September 1949. Acted in the role of Company Secretary and Cashier.

Arnold Kennerley

Joined in 1930 at the age of 14 as an office boy; worked his way through the positions of junior and senior clerk, and Office Manager until he was appointed Company Secretary and Director. Remained with the company until his retirement in 1981.

Margrete (Greta) Marks

Born in Cologne and undertook part of her training at the Bauhaus School. She established her own pottery in 1923 which, at its height, employed 120 staff. However, the increasing Nazi influence made business difficult and life dangerous for Greta and her two children. By 1935, the factory had been appropriated and she had fled the country. On reaching England, she travelled to Stoke-on-Trent where she was initially assisted by Gordon Forsyth who arranged for her to teach at the Burslem School of Art. Following a less than successful stay at Minton's, Greta established her own pottery, renting space in a number of factories. It is about this time that she also pursued freelance design work, receiving commissions from Ridgway's and E. Brain Foley China. The other manufacturers for whom she undertook work are not recorded but the anecdotal evidence strongly suggests that Fielding's was one of them.

James Sayer

Born in Yorkshire, he joined Abraham Fielding as a young man in a junior position and steadily progressed to become a director with the formation of the limited company in 1905. He stayed with the company until his death in 1922. His organising ability was proverbial and he was a much respected member of the North Staffordshire Branch of the UK Commercial Travellers' Association.

During the 1890's, as an amateur footballer, he played for a time with Stoke, eventually becoming an international. He was an ardent churchman and a Freemason.

Harvey Stonehewer

Joined in 1934 at the age of 14 as an assistant forwarding clerk. Promoted through various clerical and managerial positions in the warehouses working closely with Ned Taylor. Appointed Sales Manager upon Ned Taylor's death in 1960. Left Fielding's in 1965 to set up his own business as a wholesaler.

William Thomas

Joined in 1933 at the age of 14 and initially worked in the warehouse of the subsidiary company, Era Art Pottery. He moved to the Crown Devon warehouse approximately a year later and, at the age of 16, was placed in charge of the Scotch (sic) and Irish Section. After World War II, he became assistant to Frederick Turner, later adding management of the stores to his responsibilities which he retained upon becoming the Lodgeman. In 1953/54, he took over as the Biscuit Warehouse Manager and was also in charge of the Dipping House. He was Production Manager when he left the company in 1981.

Alfred Tomkinson

Joined in 1948 as General Manager following the death of Frederick Turner. He had wide experience of earthenware and china manufacture having previously been employed at Paragon China. He was appointed a director in September 1949.

Frederick Turner

Joined in 1916 as General Manager from a management position at James Macintyre & Co. One of his first responsibilities was the supervision of the installation of the Dressler tunnel oven which was one of the first in the Potteries. Widely respected as a knowledgeable and able potter, he was responsible for many of the outstanding glazes used by Fielding's. He remained with the company until his death in January 1948 at the age of 70.

He was a pioneer member and past President of the British Ceramic Society and lectured in ceramics in the the North Staffordshire technical schools for a number of years.

Resident Designers	**Consultant Designers**
C. Beresford-Hopkins	Kathleen Parsons
Enoch Boulton	Greta Marks
William Kemp	Robin Gray
Philip Foster	Colin Melbourne
John Cuffley	Ng Eng Teng
	E. Miles-Knowles
	J & G Morten

Modellers	**Copper Plate Engravers**
Cyril Lancaster	Ron Mayer
Leo Lewis	Eric Coates

The 'Missus' (in charge of the paintresses)

Mrs Rosoman
Dorothy Nixon

Other Characters

Cissie Jackson   in charge of the mouffle shop
Harold Toft   packer

Sales Representatives

Mr Antill
Mr H.T. Fisher
Mr H.F. McCarthy
Mr C.J. Cartlidge
Mr J. Pedder
Mr G. Schmidt
Mr M. Shaw

Mr A. Fielding	£11
Mr A.R. Fielding	£2
Mr A. Hobson	£9
Mr J. Wagstaffe	£5
Mr Turner	£7
Mr Hopkins	£10
Mr J.T. Broome	£6
Mr E. Goodwin	£4
Mr Slater	£4
Mr E. Taylor	£3
Mr J. Kittridge	£3 10/-
Mr F. Lidgett	£4
Mr Darrigan	£3 10/-
Mrs Rosoman	£2
Mrs Minshull	£2 10/-
Miss Bowyer	£2 5/-
Miss Colclough	£2
Miss Hemmings	£1 14/-
Miss Clewes	£2
Miss Smith	£1 3/-
Miss Clarke	£ 19/-
Woolley	£ 15/-
Washing (Mr A.F.)	£ 10/-

Extract from Staff Salaries Book 1926

Paintresses				Ward	L.	
				Silk	M.	
Attwood	E.			Finney	O.	
Quimby	M.	60		Eccles	M.J.	
Dutton	A.M.			Moors	E.	
Haycock	E.			McMurtie	A.	
Bradley	V.			Wright	N.	
Gibson	E.			Shaw	W.	
Yorath	J.			Givilt	M.	
Palin	V.			Browning	B.	
Yates	D.			Morris	J.	
Morgan	H.			Rushton	F.	
Whittaker	R.			Beckett	H.	
Golden	S.			Smith	H.	
Mountford	H.			Jones	A.	
Deakin	S.			Clowes	G.	
Bromley	R.			Taylor	N.M.	
Moreton	M.			Platt	G.	
Graves	G.			Brown	H.	
Birks	D.			Cummings	J.	
Wilson	G.			Appleton	M.	
Green	F.			Wilcox	E.	
Clarke	L.			Wainwright	J.	
Jenks	F.			Mayer	F.	
McDermott	N.					
Moran	F.			**Men Painters**		
Dewhurst	K.					
Morris	D.			Lamonby	W.	
Farmilo	D.			Adams	L.	
Harrison	J.	17		Stockley	W.	
Worsdale	H.	17		Wilcox	T.	
Edwards	M.			Fenn	J.	
Johnson	M.			Carter	N.	
Lines	V.			Webb	A.	
Baddeley	M.	15		Gibson	G.	
Bostock	J.	15		Nixon	D.	17
Stott	E.D.	15		Reynolds	F.	
Turner	B.	15		Doroszley	D.	
Dono	J.	15				

Extract From Wages Book 1950

NOTE : It is assumed that the numbers refer to the ages of the individuals.

Agents

1895

Charles Berry
23 Thavies Inn
Holborn Circus
London

T.J. Simey
Cape Town &
Port Elizabeth
South Africa

1908

Change of London agent to C.J. Pratt

1917

Mr A. Hooper
Gamage Buildings
Holborn Circus
London

193 King Street
London
Ontario
Canada

Frank Turton
200 Castlereagh Street
Sydney
Australia

Messrs Savage & Irvine
Lima 291
Buenos Aires
Argentina

1939

A.J. Holdcroft
75 Gamage Buildings
Holborn Circus
London

A.E. Cruttenden
Beaucaire House
103 York Street
Sydney
Australia

John Raine Ltd
Laery's Building
7 Allen Street
Wellington
New Zealand

O. Hornsleth
St. Kongensgade 81
Copenhagen
Denmark

S.N. Spence
253 Sherman Ave. Sth
Hamilton
Ontario
Canada

Brown & Hargrave
321 Water Street
Vancouver
Canada

L.A. Solomon
8 Progress Lane
off Strand Street
P.O. Box 267
Capetown
South Africa

S. Morel
39/41 Bradlow's Buildings
corner Market & Von Brandis Streets
Johannesburg
South Africa

1950

A.J. Holdcroft
72/3 Gamage Buildings
Holborn Circus
London

A.E. Cruttenden
Beaucaire House
103 York Street
Sydney
Australia

J. Raine Ltd
Laery's Building
7 Allen Street
Wellington
New Zealand

L.A. Solomon
8 Progress Lane
off Strand Street
Cape Town
South Africa

Fondeville & Co Inc
149/151 Fifth Avenue
New York 10
USA

Cesar Rosa
Av. Quintana 416 - Piso 6
Buenos Aires
Argentina

Oscar Hornsleth
Store Kongensgade 81
Copenhagen
Denmark

Paul Brieven
Avenue de la Reine 49
Brussels
Belgium

A. Pfister
6 Avenue Fraisse
Lausanne
Switzerland

Emilio Fischer
Viale Bianca
Marias 23
          Milan
Italy

Leo Preuss
Apartado 339
San Jose
Costa Rica

H.J.J. Evans
C/o Messrs J. Butler
292 Kingsway
Valletta
Malta

Emerson Nichols Agencies
London
Ontario
Canada

G. Lindley & Co Ltd
St Andrews House
Holborn Circus
London
(For Hong Kong, Singapore & Malaya)

1959
Change of London agent to Vernon Soleil.

1971
Change of London agent to J.H. Service & Sons.

Appendix C : Bibliography

Ceramic Art Of Great Britain
Llewellyn Jewitt

People Of The Potteries, A Dictionary Of Local Biography
Edited by Denis Stuart; Department of Adult Education, University of Keele

Majolica, A Complete History And Illustrated Survey
Marilyn G. Karmason & Joan B. Stacke; Harry N. Abrams Inc, New York

Majolica, British Continental And American Wares 1851 - 1915
Victoria Bergesen; Barrie & Jenkins

Majolica
Nicholas M. Dawes; Crown Publishers Inc, New York

The Crown Devon Story
Ray Barker; R.B. Publications

The Shorter Connection, A Family Pottery 1874 - 1974
Irene & Gordon Hopwood; Richard Dennis

Dynamic Design, The British Pottery Industry 1940 - 1990
Kathy Niblett; Stoke-on-Trent City Museum & Art Gallery

Twentieth Century Design : Ceramics
Francis Hannah; Bell & Hyman

Encyclopedia Of British Pottery & Porcelain Marks
Geoffrey Godden; Barrie & Jenkins

Handbook Of Pottery & Porcelain Marks
J.P. Cushion; Faber & Faber

Greta Pottery
Pat Halfpenny; Northern Ceramic Society Journal Number 8, 1991

Periodicals

Pottery Gazette & Glass Trade Review
Pottery Gazette & Glass Trade Review Directory & Yearbook
Pottery & Glass Record
Crockery & Glass Journal
Cox's Potteries Annual & Yearbook
Evening Sentinel, Stoke-on-Trent

Appendix D : Pattern Reference Guide

This appendix provides summaries of pattern numbers together with further details of significant ranges. Unfortunately, due to the prolific output of the pottery and the incompleteness of the records, it has not been possible to give complete listings.

Pattern Numbers

The majority of pieces produced by S. Fielding & Co carry a painted or printed pattern number on their base and, in some instances, a pattern name. By using the lists given below, in conjunction with the backstamps, approximate dates of articles may be ascertained.

The lists have been compiled primarily from the original pattern books, supplemented by information gathered from the trade press and other contemporary sources. It is important to remember that the date a design was entered into the pattern books does not necessarily indicate the date of manufacture which, particularly for a popular pattern, could have been considerably later. Unfortunately, the pattern books are incomplete, some are in poor condition and many patterns are undated. However, the first dated pattern number for each year is given, wherever possible.

The first pattern book available commences at pattern X1, dated March 1898. The numbering runs consecutively through to X999 at which point, the 'X' prefix is dropped and it would appear that the intention was to replace it by a '1'. Hence the numbers would have continued as 1001, 1002 etc. However, this was not implemented resulting in patterns being numbered as 001, 002 etc. This revised system runs consecutively to pattern number 3386 which is dated October 1946.

X1	Mar	1898	1074	Jul	1918
X48	Jan	1899	1098	Feb	1919
X131	Jan	1900	1131	Sep	1920
X313	Jan	1901	1138	Feb	1921
X429	Jan	1902	1170	Mar	1922
X569	Jan	1903	1268	Jan	1923
X705	Feb	1904	1332	Jan	1924
X811	Jan	1905	1636	Dec	1925
X915	Jan	1906	1663	Aug	1926
028	Jan	1907	1700	Jan	1927
0233	Feb	1908	2051	Jan	1930
0318	Jan	1909	2229	Sep	1932
0493	Feb	1910	2417	Apr	1933
0596	Jan	1911	2489	Oct	1933
0693	Apr	1912	2691	Jul	1935
0755	Jan	1913	3193	Mar	1939
0907	Jan	1914	3306	May	1940
0979	Feb	1915	3344	Feb	1941
1006	Apr	1916	3370	Mar	1942
1035	Jan	1917	3386	Oct	1946

In November 1944, a new pattern numbering system was instigated with numbers starting at 1001. This was obviously used concurrently with the existing main pattern book since, as has been previously indicated, patterns were entered in that book up to October 1946. No rationale for the new numbering system has been identified but it continued to operate until January 1963 when the last design, number 1413, was entered. Few dates are recorded, those available are, as follows :

1001	Nov 1944	1381	Nov 1960
1012	Feb 1945	1384	Mar 1961
1269	Jan 1957	1413	Jan 1963

Obviously, care must be taken not to confuse these numbers with the much earlier main sequence numbers. However, the type of decoration together with the accompanying backstamp should prove a reliable guide.

To add further to the confusion, another new pattern book started in approximately 1950 with numbers from 5001 onwards. Patterns were entered into this book up until approximately 1969, the last number being 6393. Hence, this book was also in use at the same time as the one with patterns in the 1000 series.

5001	c. 1950	5828	Apr 1961
5061	c. 1950	5971	May 1962
5385	c. 1955	6021	Jan 1963
5481	Nov 1956	6091	Feb 1964
5518	Feb 1957	6118	Apr 1967
5568	Oct 1957	6268	Dec 1967
5665	Apr 1959	6370	c. 1968/69
5735	Jan 1960	6393	c. 1969

Separate pattern books were used for particular classes of ware, denoted by a letter prefix. The following have been identified :

Prefix 'A'	Handpainted, often executed by apprentices
Prefix 'M'	Matt glazes
Prefix 'D'	Dinnerwares
Prefix 'C'	China

'A'Patterns

Pattern numbers with an 'A' prefix were used in the early 1900's but no details of these are available. It would appear that this numbering method was re-introduced in the late 1920's and probably started at A1. The lowest known pattern number from this period is A19 which is a bold geometric design of overlapping circles intersected by chevrons. However, the pattern book does not start until number A228 and then runs consecutively to the final pattern of A736. Although very few dates are recorded, the style of the designs indicates a period from the early 1930's whilst the last patterns were entered in 1942.

'M' Patterns

Reference is made in the pattern books to a matt pattern book. However, this book is not available in the archives. From the style of the designs known from actual pieces, it is likely that these pattern numbers were used from the early 1930's through to the mid 1940's. The lowest known number is M32 which is a flower border decoration on a yellow ground.

'D' Patterns

The dinnerware patterns were entered at the back of the 'A' pattern book. Numbers commence at D333 which relates to the Beverley shape indicating a late 1930's date. The last number is D511 which is dated February 1942. No further information is available.

'C' Patterns

Pattern numbers with a 'C' prefix indicate a china, rather than earthenware, body (see China section). The following details are taken from a pattern book listing entitled 'Tea Sets China Cups'.

C101	May	C109	Spring
C102	Spring	C110	May
C103	Ascot	C111	Evas
C104	Old Bow	C112	Rex
C105	Lotus	C113	Oban
C106	Windsor	C114	Etna
C107	Salop	C115	Peel
C108	Lace		

Shape Numbers and Names

In addition to the pattern number, many pieces also have a moulded model or shape number and/or name on the base. These are often difficult to read but can provide an extra interesting detail. Shape names known to have been incorporated in this way include Louis, Queen Anne, Hurley and Eros.

From the mid 1940's, new shapes had numbers prefixed with an 'A'.

Royal Chelsea Patterns

Number	Pattern
1	Poppy
2	Blossom
3	Lily
4	Tulip
5	Iris
6	Convolvulus
7	Pansy
8	Lotus
9	Carnation (Royal Oxford)
10	Orchid
11	Orchid (gold background)
12	Begonia
13	Iceland Poppy
14	No details
15	No details
16	No details
17	No details
18	Chrysanthemum
19	Spanish Iris
20	Australian Pompon

Royal Guelph Patterns

Number	Pattern
1/1	Monk looking to left
1/2	Monk looking to right
2/1	Dutch girl
2/2	Dutch boy
3/1	Jester looking to left
3/2	Jester looking to right
4/1	Dutch man
4/2	Dutch woman
5/1	Monk with book
6/1	Girl with rake
6/2	Man with sythe
7/1	Old sailor
7/2	No details
8/1	Cattle looking to left
8/2	Cattle looking to right
9/1	No details
9/2	No details
10/1	No details
10/2	No details
11/1	Smoker (tobacco jar)
12/1	Witch
12/2	Miser
13/1	Man with sickle
13/2	Girl with fork
14/1	Japanese girl looking to left
14/2	Japanese girl looking to right
15/1	Watchman

Summary of Artist's Patterns

Pattern	Date	Pattern Name	Artist
0112	1907	Wild Rose	
0279	1908	Wild Rose	
0670	1911	Game (Pheasants)	J. Coleman
0671	1911	Game	
0681	1911/12	Devonia (Roses)	G. Cox
0682		Peacock	H. Stuart
			W. Stuart
0685		Ducks	
0694	1912	Storks	Lewis
			A. Marsh
0735	1912	Sheep	F. Hancock
0766	1913	Goose Girl	
0782	1913	Storks	
0783	1913	Scotch Cattle	G. Cox
0790	1913	Scotch Cattle	
0829	1913	New Game	
0830	1913	New Game (Pheasants)	W. Lamonby
0856	1914	Wild Ducks	
0857	1914	Storks	
0865	1914	Pheasants	
0929	1914	Dogs (Setters)	R. Hinton
1072	1921	Fruit	F. Cole
1137	1921	Stags	G. Cox
1272	1923	Scotch Cattle	
1666	1926	Saxon Roses	
1667	1926	Saxon Roses	
1834		S.A. Scenes	
2700	1935/36	Duck	W. Lamonby
2701	1935/36	Grouse	W. Lamonby
2702	1935/36	Pheasant	W. Lamonby
3046		Tally-Ho (Hunting Scene)	W. Lamonby
3047		Pheasants	W. Lamonby
3349	1941	Dogs	W. Lamonby
3350	1941	Pheasants	W. Lamonby
3351	1941	Hunting Scene	W. Lamonby
3352	1941	Roll Out The Barrel	W. Lamonby

Ivrine Figures

Number	Figure
1	Dog with bird on stand
2	Stork, right hand
3	Stork, left hand
4	Cockerel
5	Elephant
6	Newfoundland
7	John Bull
8	Water Carrier
9	Officer
10	Fox
11	Victorian jug
12	Flower girl
13	Dancing girl
14	Lady with jar
15	Lady with jar and flowers
16	No details
17	Gainsborough girl
18	Greek lady
19	Lady de Bath
20	Italian woman
21	Italian man
22	Peace
23	Vanity
24	Lady sitting (tray)
25	Lady reclining (tray)
26	Lady dancer (large)
27	Bowl with lady in centre

Lustrine

Number	Pattern
1	Queen of Fairies
2	Mermaids
3	Dragon
4	Lizard
5	Chameleon
6	No details
7	Mosaic centre
8	Fish and ships
9	Leopards
10	Birds

Particulars of Numbers for Lustrine Grounds

Number	Details
L1	Saxe-blue
2	Purple
3	Orange
4	Light green
5	Yellow; pearline inside
6	Light green; pearline inside
7	Dark green; orange inside
8	Purple; light green inside
9	Saxe-blue; pearline inside
10	Orange; pearline inside
11	Stippled oven blue; solid on-glaze; pearline all over
12	Stippled and blown blue outside on-glaze; pearline inside
13	Purple; pearline inside
14	Blue under-glaze; pearline inside and outside
15	Mauve under-glaze; pink inside
16	Pink
17	Orange; mother-of-pearl finish
18	Purple; mother-of-pearl finish
19	Light green; mother-of-pearl finish
20	Dark green; mother-of-pearl finish
21	Yellow; mother-of-pearl finish
22	Mauve; mother-of-pearl finish
23	Pink; mother-of-pearl finish
24	Saxe-blue; mother-of-pearl finish
25	Royal purple; mother-of-pearl finish
26	Mottled blue; yellow inside
27	Stippled under-glaze black; solid ruby lustre (3 coats)
28	Stippled under-glaze black; blown under-glaze blue; mother-of-pearl finish

29	Stippled under-glaze pink; broken blue lustre
30	Stippled under-glaze black; solid ruby lustre (3 coats); best gold
31	'Lucien' broken lustre
32	No details
33	No details
34	No details
35	As L17 outside; solid black inside
36	As L19 outside; solid black inside
37	Seagulls; printed in black, stencilled and blown in saxe-blue; yellow inside; gold edge
38	Seagulls; printed in black, stencilled and blown in green; orange inside; mother-of-pearl finish
39	As L38 with orange outside, green inside
40	As L38 with pink outside, mauve inside
41	Plain lustre, green; orange inside; black edge
42	Plain lustre, saxe-blue; yellow inside
43	Plain lustre, orange; saxe-blue inside
44	Blossom; printed in black, under-glaze blue and green; orange lustre finish; black edge
45	As L44 in pink and green; lemon lustre finish
46	As L44, stencilled and blown in green; coloured in pink and dark green; mother-of-pearl finish
47	Dragonfly; printed in black, under-glaze in pink, green, dark green, black, yellow; stippled softly and lightly in black; stencilled and blown in pink; pearline and registered gold print. Open pieces to have gold rose spray border and gold edge
48	As L47, coloured in under-glaze green, orange, brown; stippled in black; stencilled and blown in blue. Leaves filled-in in red
49	New Tropical; printed in black, coloured in blue, green, orange and dark green; stippled black; ruby lustre (3 coats); registered gold print and gold bamboo border, gold edge
50	Pencilled black under-glaze band; one coat orange lustre all over. Laurel wreath printed in best gold on band with liquid gold band, line and edge
51	Plain lustre, pink; mauve inside
52	Stippled and blown oven blue; butterflys printed in gold; pearlined and filled up in purple lustre; liquid gold edge (1 fire)
53	Dragonfly; printed in black, coloured in greens, fawn, pink and blue; stippled and blown; finished as Rural
54	Stippled and blown oven blue, as L12. Printed moss rose chintz in gold with liquid gold edge (1 fire)
55	Plain lustre, orange; green inside; black edge
56	Dragons; printed in smoke, filled up solid in green; stencilled and blown in oven blue. Dragons registered in gold; gold edge

57	Pagoda; printed in black, coloured in green, dark green and oven blue; stippled in black; ruby ground. Registered in gold, tangerine lustre; best gold edge
58	Ships; printed in black; pencilled and shaded in black; orange lustre ground; black edge (1 fire)
59	Blossom, as L44 inside only but mother-of-pearl inside instead of orange lustre
60	Mavis Bird; printed in pearl, coloured in pink, green, yellow and blue. Mixed green leaves; printed border; orange outside, mother-of-pearl inside; black edge
61	Fruit Wreath; border printed in pearl, coloured in pink, green, yellow; lined under pattern; stippled outside, mother-of-pearl finish
62	Filey; printed in pearl (3 sprays); stippled cantonon pattern; coloured in green, blue, pink and yellow; green outside, mother-of-pearl finish, black edge
63	Birds and Mountain; printed in black, shaded in black; orange lustre ground, black edge (1 fire)
64	Filey, as L62, with pink outside in place of green
65	Roslyn; roses printed in black; painted roses and leaves; blown oven blue from top, medium strength shading to white at bottom. Roses only cleaned out; one coat of ruby; edged in blue
66	Blossom and Birds on ruby lustre ground; 'Norfolk'
67	Roses, as L65, orange lustre in place of ruby
68	Delphinium; ruby
69	Chinese Panel
70	Swallows, as L52
71	Mavis Bird; plum lustre ground
72	English Castles; printed in black; stippled in black; orange lustre
73	South American Views; ruby lustre ground
74	Woodland (2133); orange lustre ground
75	Sylvan; matt glaze green ground
76	Exotic Bird (2130); orange lustre ground
77	Exotic Bird (2130); ruby lustre ground
78	As 2072; ruby lustre ground
79	Coffees, as L23; mauve, solid gold inside; gold edge, handle and foot line
80	Orange lustre; mother-of-pearl inside; black edge
81	Lemon lustre; mother-of-pearl inside; black edge
82	Orange lustre top half, mother-of-pearl bottom half and inside; black edge and line
83	Mother-of-pearl from bottom; orange lustre points from top; edged in black; mother-of-pearl inside
84	Orange and lemon lustre in alternate Brick pattern; mother-of-pearl inside; black edge
85	Bird and Rockery; ruby lustres

86	Filey; printed in black, coloured under-glaze with stippled pink, orange lustres ground. Flowers and Rococo border traced in gold, best gold star centre and edge
87	Arch; printed in canton, coloured under-glaze; four small sprays, black band; stippled pink, orange lustre ground. Mother-of-pearl inside over top trellis border; gold print, best gold edge
88	Filey; printed border in black, coloured under-glaze with stippled pale blue; mother-of-pearl inside, deep turquoise outside. Relief enamel round top of border; illuminated and star centre; best gold edge
89	Coffees; stippled under-glaze pink; orange lustre (2 coats); gold line and handle
90	Coffees; blown under-glaze green; mother-of-pearl; gold line and handle
91	Coffees; blown under-glaze pink; mother-of-pearl; gold line and handle
92	Coffees; blown under-glaze dark blue; mother-of-pearl; gold line and handle
93	Coffees; under-glaze green outside, lemon inside; mother-of-pearl; gold handle and edge
94	June; printed in pink, painted in greens, pink, blue and yellow; border pencilled in black; stippled pink, orange lustre ground; gold print border and pattern; best gold edge and foot
95	No details
96	New Flowers; printed in black, coloured under-glaze; gold print Dahlia (2343); orange lustre
97	Butterfly, as L52; printed and painted in black; stippled pink, orange lustre ground; liquid gold finish; enamelled red, gold registered
98	As L74; ruby ground
99	As Sylvan, no butterflys, straps border only; best gold inside and finish
100	Fantasia; printed in black, enamelled in assorted colours; stippled pink, orange lustre ground; gold print and relief enamels; mother-of-pearl and gold bead inside; best gold edge; black bead outside
101	As L97, with gold print Bird and Floral spray as L70; under-glaze pink and pink stipple
102	Ruby lustre, stippled black under-glaze with printed gold mosaic border (2114); gold lined, solid gold handle and edge
103	Ruby lustre; gold mosaic border
104	Under-glaze dark oven blue; printed gold mosaic border; gold lined, solid gold handle and edge
105	As L99, green instead of ruby
106	Best coffees, Mayfair; as L99 but mother-of-pearl inside; best gold finish

107	Best coffees, Mayfair; as L102 but mother-of-pearl inside; best gold finish
108	Best coffees, Mayfair; as L104 but mother-of-pearl inside; best gold finish
109	No details
110	Coffeeware; green lustre, Sylvan border only as L105 but liquid gold inside and finish
111	Coffeeware; under-glaze dark oven blue; printed liquid gold mosaic border as L104 but liquid gold inside and finish
112	Coffeeware; as L108 but maroon; gold mosaic border; mother-of-pearl inside, gold finish
113	As L112 but under-glaze black; mother-of-pearl inside
114	As L112 but groundlaid green; mother-of-pearl inside

Summary of Nurseryware Patterns

Pattern	Date	Description
X217	1900	Greenaway litho figure subjects
X487	1902	Greenaway litho subjects
X699	1905	Maypole
X707	1905	Puppy and ducks
X725	1905	Horse subjects
X839	1905	Cats and basket
X853	1905	Greenaway litho figure subjects
0267	1908	Hunting subjects
0440	1910	Teddy bears
2205	1932	Fairies, baby subjects
2489	1933	Fairy litho (special set)
2490	1933	Zoo series, various animals
2491	1933	Tommy Tucker litho
2492	1933	Little Miss Muffet (Joan Harris)
2493	1933	Boy Blue and Curly Locks litho
2569	1934	Lambs and rabbits
3129	1938	Nursery rhymes; Cat and The Fiddle
3336	1940/41	Ride-a-Cock-Horse
3366	1941	Little Bo-Peep
5610	1957/58	Animals playing on the beach
	1978/79	Chickadee

Index

215